EARLY YEARS

AROUND THE YEAR

14 APR

25 FEB

17 OC

Creative
development
Seasonal activities

Jenni Tavener

WITHDRAWN

D1422176

Seasonal ideas • Festivals • Early learning goals

CREDITS

British Library Cataloguing-in-Publication Data
A catalogue record for this book is available from the British Library.

ISBN 0 439 01910 9

AUTHOR
Jenni Tavener

EDITOR
Lesley Sudlow

ASSISTANT EDITOR
Saveria Mezzana

SERIES DESIGNER
Anna Oliwa

DESIGNER
Paul Roberts

ILLUSTRATIONS
Jenny Tulip

COVER ILLUSTRATION
Anna Hopkins

DEDICATION
To Jessica Holmes

ACKNOWLEDGEMENTS
The publishers gratefully acknowledge permission to reproduce the following copyright material:

Brenda Williams for 'Autumn changes' by Brenda Williams © 2001, Brenda Williams, previously unpublished.

Text © 2001 Jenni Tavener
© 2001 Scholastic Ltd

Published by Scholastic Ltd, Villiers House, Clarendon Avenue, Leamington Spa, Warwickshire CV32 5PR

Designed using Adobe Pagemaker
Printed by Proost NV, Belgium

Visit our website at www.scholastic.co.uk

1 2 3 4 5 6 7 8 9 0   1 2 3 4 5 6 7 8 9 0

CONTENTS

Around the year

The aims of the series

This book forms part of a series of six books covering the six areas of learning and provides activities to support the Early Learning Goals (QCA). They offer practitioners working with young children a wide range of activities to use throughout the year that are linked to seasonal and festival-based themes.

Creative development

The main aim of this book is to provide a wide range of activities to help develop children's creative skills and imagination. Activities to encourage art and craft include opportunities to design, construct or decorate a range of pictures, models, paintings, displays, mobiles, jewellery, cards and keepsakes. There are also activity ideas to inspire role-play, music, poetry and dance to help further explore the seasons and festivals, for example, using crowns and masks for re-enacting multicultural stories, making a large 3-D structure to represent a dragon boat for imaginative play, and using a wide range of instruments to sing and adapt weather-themed songs.

About the book

Each chapter is based on one of the four seasons and provides activities that explore all aspects of creative development. Each chapter comprises fourteen activities including six based around seasons and eight focusing on seasonal festivals. The learning objectives for these activities are all linked to the Early Learning Goals (QCA). The ideas suggested can be applied equally well to the documents on pre-school education published for Scotland, Wales and Northern Ireland.

How to use this book

On pages 7 and 8, you will find a summary of information about the festivals covered in this book. The format for each activity is the same throughout the book. First, a 'Learning objective' gives the key skills that the children will be developing. Each activity gives the group size, details of resources needed and any necessary preparation required. Where an activity involves handling of food, this symbol (!) will

remind you to check for any allergies and dietary requirements. The activities themselves are described under the heading 'What to do'. Although they are aimed at four-year-olds, the 'Support' section gives suggestions about how the main activity can be adapted for younger children or those with special needs, and the 'Extension' section explains how the main activity can be extended for older or more able children. The 'Home links' section offers relevant ways to involve parents and carers in their children's learning.

How to use the photocopiable sheets

This book provides 16 photocopiable sheets to support or extend the main activities. They include a range of poems, a story, a song and stencils.

Links with home

It is very important to establish a positive liaison between home and early years settings. Involve parents and carers as much as possible with the themes and activities organized for the children – for example, provide a brief list for each half term outlining the multicultural festivals that you hope to cover with the children.

Invite parents and carers in to share their personal, firsthand experiences of the multicultural celebrations. Some may even have relevant photographs, costumes or examples of decorations that they could show to the children. Good communication between home and your setting will help lead to a greater awareness and understanding of the children's needs and interests, and will enrich the children's learning due

to the extra input offered by their parents or carers.

Links with other areas of the curriculum

There are many opportunities during the creative activities in this book to link in other curriculum areas. Personal, social and emotional development is addressed by providing opportunities for the children to work as a team during role-play, co-operate with one another during shared model-making activities, and establish a positive self image when personal artwork is displayed.

Communication, language and literacy goes hand-in-hand with creative activities as the children are surrounded by interesting and colourful experiences which help to promote discussion, verbal responses and the sharing of views and ideas. Reading and writing opportunities arise naturally due to the children's own enthusiasm to label artwork, write in greetings cards and create letters, notes or messages during imaginative play situations.

Practical challenges to inspire mathematical development are offered in activities that involve making and using 2-D and 3-D shapes. Mathematical resources for comparing and matching can be made or used in activities such as 'Tall, textured sunflower' on page 9 and 'Weather chart' on page 53. The activities 'Ten white snowflakes' on page 56 and 'Giant Advent calendar' on page 57 can be used to help counting skills and number recognition.

Themes to encourage knowledge and understanding of the world are offered throughout the book in activities that explore the weather, colours in nature and the use of patterns or symbols in festival celebrations.

Overall, the book aims to provide enjoyable and educational opportunities in creative development and to offer activities which can also be used to encourage co-operation, sharing, taking turns and teamwork.

Festivals

St David's Day (1 March)
A Welsh celebration of its patron saint, involving traditional Welsh music and songs. People wear the national symbols of the leek and daffodil.

Purim (March)
A Jewish festival remembering Queen Esther who saved the lives of Jewish people in Persia. Presents are given and children attend fancy-dress parties.

Mother's Day (March/April)
Once a holiday for servant girls to visit their mothers with gifts, it is now a time to show love and thanks to mothers.

Easter (March/April)
The most important Christian festival when Jesus' return to life is celebrated. People give chocolate eggs as a symbol of new life.

Baisakhi (14 April)
The Sikh New Year festival commemorating the five volunteers that offered to sacrifice themselves at Guru Gobind Singh's request. A vegetarian meal is often shared.

St George's Day (23 April)
An English celebration of its patron saint. The story of George and the Dragon is remembered when St George slayed a dragon.

Hanamatsuri (April)
A Japanese flower festival celebrating the birth of Buddha. Baby Buddha images are placed in floral shrines symbolizing the garden in which the Buddha was born.

May Day (1 May)
May Day celebrates the goddess Flora. Traditions include dancing around a maypole, processions and selecting a May Queen.

Wesak (May/June)
Theravada Buddhists celebrate the birth, enlightenment and death of the Buddha on this day. People decorate their temples and homes with candles, flowers and incense.

Shavuot (May/June)
A Jewish festival celebrating the revelation of the Ten Commandments to Moses on Mount Sinai. Synagogues are decorated with dairy foods and fruit.

Midsummer's Day (24 June)
Falls shortly after the longest day of the year. Traditions include bonfires, feasts and torchlit processions.

Father's Day (June)
Children give love and thanks to their fathers during this modern festival.

Dragon Boat Festival (June)
A Chinese festival honouring Ch'u Yuan who drowned himself in protest of the Emperor. Today dragon boat races symbolize the rush to save him.

St Swithun's Day (15 July)
Legend says that if it rains on this day, it will do so for 40 days and nights.

Raksha Bandhan (July/August)
A Hindu festival when girls tie a rakhi (bracelet) around their brothers' wrists to protect them, and the brothers promise to protect their sisters.

Janamashtami (July/August/ September)
A Hindu festival celebrating the birth of Krishna with festivities beginning at midnight, the time of Krishna's birth.

Rosh Hashana (September)
This festival celebrates the Jewish New Year. People reflect on their behaviour over the past year and send cards.

Grandparent's Day (September)
A modern festival in which children and families thank their grandparents by making cards and sending them gifts.

Sukkot (September/October)
A Jewish festival that commemorates the people's journey in the wilderness after escaping from Egypt. Temporary shelters are built and harvest is celebrated.

Harvest Festival (September/October)
A time of thanksgiving for the harvesting of crops. Traditions include harvest suppers and giving of food to the needy.

Divali (October/November)
Hindus remember the story of Rama and Sita. Sikhs celebrate the sixth Guru, Guru Hargobind's escape from imprisonment. People decorate their homes with divas (lamps).

Bonfire Night (5 November)
Fireworks are set off to remember the time when Guy Fawkes tried, but failed, to blow up the Houses of Parliament with gunpowder.

St Andrew's Day (30 November)
A Scottish celebration of their patron saint. A traditional meal of haggis, neeps and tatties is eaten by many families.

Hanukkah (November/December)
A Jewish festival of light lasting eight days, commemorating the reclamation of the temple from the Syrians and the miracle of the temple light that burned for eight days on a small amount of oil.

Advent (December)
Christian period of preparation for Jesus' birth, beginning on the fourth Sunday before Christmas and ending on Christmas Day. Traditions include Advent candles and calendars.

Christmas Day (25 December)
Christian festival celebrating the birth of Jesus. People decorate their homes and exchange gifts as a reminder of those given to Jesus.

Eid-ul-Fitr (December/January)
Muslim festival held at the end of Ramadan. People wear new clothes, visit family and friends, exchange gifts and eat a celebratory meal together.

New Year (1 January)
New Year is celebrated with parties and the traditional singing of 'Auld Lang Syne' at midnight on 31 December. People reflect on the past and make resolutions for the future.

Saraswati Puja (January)
This Hindu festival is associated with Saraswati, the goddess of learning and the arts. It marks the start of spring in India when the fields are full of yellow flowers.

Chinese New Year (January/February)
The most important Chinese festival, lasting 15 days. People clean and decorate their homes, wear new clothes, visit family and friends and exchange gifts with each other.

Valentine's Day (14 February)
The patron saint of lovers' day is celebrated by sending anonymous cards and gifts to loved ones. It is thought that Valentine was probably a roman soldier that refused to agree not to marry.

Shrove Tuesday (February/March)
This day is also known as 'Pancake Day'. It is celebrated 46 days before Easter Sunday. Pancakes are made to signify the beginning of the fast of Lent.

Tall, textured sunflower

What you need
A variety of yellow, green and brown materials with different textures such as silky smooth fabric, bumpy corrugated card, furry material, wrinkled tissue paper and so on; glue; scissors; a long strip of paper or card approximately 30cm x 100cm; pictures of, or a real, sunflower; sunflower seeds; name labels.

Preparation
Draw the outline of a simple sunflower head at the top of the strip of paper with a long, thick stalk and several leaves reaching down to the bottom of the paper.

What to do
Show the children the sunflower seeds. Explain to them that when the seeds are planted and cared for, they grow into tall sunflowers. Look at the pictures of a sunflower. Tell the children that sunflowers can grow as tall as them, and sometimes, as tall as adults.

Invite the children to help you create a tall sunflower picture that can be used as a height chart. Give them the strip of card showing the sunflower outline, together with a wide variety of textured materials in shades of yellow and brown. Encourage them to feel the different textures, and help them to cut small 'swatches' of each material to glue onto the sunflower head.

When the children have finished making the sunflower head, provide a variety of textured materials in shades of green and ask the group to decorate the stalk and leaves with these.

When the sunflower is complete, mount it on the wall and invite each child to attach their name label next to the sunflower to mark their own height. Use the sunflower for matching and comparing activities and to inspire mathematical language such as 'smaller than', 'taller than', 'as tall as', 'tallest', 'shortest', 'higher than', 'lower than' and so on.

Support
Provide pre-cut swatches of material for the children to feel and glue.

Extension
Invite the children to help draw the sunflower outline.

Learning objective
To explore texture and space.

Group size
Small groups.

Home links
Prepare for the activity in advance by asking parents and carers for contributions of textured materials. Invite parents and carers in to help the children plant sunflower seeds.

Weather mobile

What you need
Circles of paper approximately 30cm in diameter; paints; paintbrushes; a window at the children's height; aprons; string; large PE hoop.

around the room, or make one long mobile by hanging all the pictures one beneath the other.

Alternatively, tie the pictures around a large PE hoop to create a weather mobile. Hang the mobile within easy reach of the children and use it to inspire discussion about the different types of weather that they have seen during the week. Invite the children to talk about their favourite weather conditions or to recall memorable events such as playing in the snow, stamping in puddles, waking in the sunshine and so on.

Sing some weather-themed songs and rhymes with the children, for example, 'Dr Foster', 'The Sun Has Got His Hat On' and 'Incy Wincy Spider'.

Invite the children to paint pictures about the rhymes. Hang these around the room with the mobiles.

What to do
Every day for a week, take the children outside and talk to them about the weather. Ask if it is sunny, wet, windy and so on. Back inside, give each child a disc of paper and some paints and encourage them to paint a picture to record the day's weather.

At the end of the week, help the children to glue their pictures back to back, and to tape a length of string to the top of each double-sided picture. Hang the pictures at varying heights

Support
Invite the children to paint blocks of colour or scribbles to represent the weather. For example, they could paint a disc yellow for a sunny day, a disc blue for a wet day or colourful scribbles for a windy day.

Extension
Provide the children with thin paintbrushes so that they can add details to their paintings, for example, people, puddles, raindrops and so on.

Spring is here!

What you need
A safe area outside where plants and minibeasts can be observed; extra adult helpers; large safety magnifying glasses; clipboards; pencils; the photocopiable sheet on page 65; plastic wallets; clip folder.

Preparation
Make a copy of the photocopiable sheet for each child.

What to do
With adult supervision, give each child large safety magnifying glasses and take them outside to observe signs of spring, for example, young plants or shoots, minibeasts, blossom, new leaves and so on. Encourage the children to talk about their observations and help them to appreciate the beauty of nature.

Give each child a clipboard, pencil and a copy of the photocopiable sheet

and ask them to draw their springtime observations. When they have completed this task, invite the children to place their drawings into individual plastic wallets that can then be put into a clip folder.

Encourage the children to think of a title for the folder, such as 'Nature drawings' or 'Springtime pictures'. The children's new pictures can then be added as the season progresses.

Support
Encourage the children to focus on making observations and talking about what they have seen instead of drawing pictures.

Extension
Encourage the children to use the magnifying glasses to help them observe and draw details such as petals and veins on leaves.

Old MacDonald's farm

What you need

A sheet of coloured A1 card; two sheets of coloured A1 paper; glue; sheets of A3 and A4 paper; paints; paintbrushes; pictures or photographs of farm animals with their young; aprons; stapler (for adult use only); black marker pen.

Preparation

Make a blank big book by folding two sheets of A1 paper inside a sheet of folded A1 card. Staple along the fold. Using a black marker pen, write 'Old MacDonald had a farm' on the cover and 'E-i-e-i-o' on the inside. On the first page write, 'And on that farm he had some...'. Leave the rest of the pages blank.

What to do

Look together at the pictures of the farm animals and their young. Sing the song 'Old MacDonald Had a Farm' with the children, ensuring that you include the names of the baby animals as well as those of the adult animals. For example, you could sing 'Old MacDonald had a farm, E-i-e-i-o, and on that farm he had some sheep and lambs, E-i-e-i-o'.

Provide each child with some paper and paints. Invite them to use the pictures and photographs of farm animals as a guide to paint a picture of one of the animals in the song.

When the children have finished, invite them to help stick the animal pictures onto the coloured pages within the big book, using a different page for each species and its young. Label each page according to the pictures, for example, 'Cows and calves', 'Sheep and lambs' and so on. Use the completed big book as a visual resource when singing as a group.

Sing an alternative version of 'Old MacDonald' with the children, for example, 'Old MacDonald had a farm, E-i-e-i-o, And on that farm he had... 5 pigs, 4 cows, 3 ducks, 2 horses and 1 dog..., E-i-e-i-o'. Encourage the children to make up their own list of animals. The numbers can be increased or reduced depending on the ability of the children.

Further adaptations to the song can be made, for example, 'Old MacDonald had a zoo' or 'Old MacDonald had some pets' and so on.

Support

Draw animal outlines for the children to paint. Encourage them to look at the pictures and photographs of animals to help them select appropriate colours and patterns for each animal.

Extension

Encourage the children to help you write the wording to the song in the big book.

Jack and the beanstalk

What you need
The story of 'Jack and the Beanstalk' (traditional); a sheet of plain fabric or an old sheet, large enough to cover a door or fill a door frame; green paint; large sponges approximately 10cm x 20cm; large paintbrushes; shallow tray; aprons; pegs or masking tape; real beans.

Preparation
If space allows, peg or tape the whole length of fabric to a table or the floor. If space is limited, the fabric can be painted in sections. Trim the large sponges into simple leaf shapes.

Learning objectives
To work creatively on a large scale; to play co-operatively as part of a group to act out a narrative.

Group size
Small groups.

What to do
Read the story of 'Jack and the Beanstalk' to the children. Discuss with them the fact that plants in real life can also grow from beans or seeds, and invite them to look at some real beans. Explain that in reality they take more than one night to grow. Tell the children that you are going to save the beans for planting at a later date.

Invite the children to help paint and print a very tall beanstalk along the large sheet of fabric. Provide each child with a large paintbrush and some green paint and encourage them to take turns at painting a long, vertical, thick line along the centre of the fabric to represent a stalk.

Next, invite the children to use the large sponges to print leaf shapes along the stalk, and leave to dry. (If painting in sections, leave the first part to dry before repeating the activity on the second section.)

When the beanstalk is complete, hang it over a safe doorway or on a wall. Invite the children to use the painting as a backdrop to inspire groups to act out the story of 'Jack and the Beanstalk'.

Support
Invite the children to put on dressing-up clothes to help them feel in character during the role-play situations.

Extension
Invite the children to take turns at being the narrator while other members of the group perform the story. Encourage the children to use a cassette recorder to record the giant saying, 'Fe, Fi, Fo, Fum' and so on.

Home links
Let the children plant some beans to take home. Invite parents and carers in to watch their children perform informal versions of 'Jack and the Beanstalk'. Ask the children to bring in story-books or pop-up books telling traditional stories.

In the garden

What you need
An area outside where spring plants and flowers can be seen, or pictures of flowers in a park or garden; several oval shapes cut from pieces of white paper approximately 15cm x 10cm; a piece of green A4 card (folded in half) for each child; scissors; colouring materials; glue.

Preparation
Cut four slits across the fold in the green card. Open the folded card and refold the two cut-out strips to create two 'pop-up' sections.

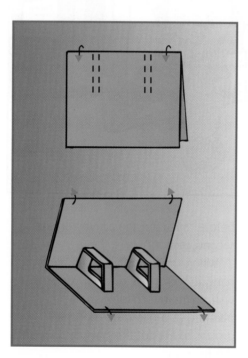

What to do
Take the children to a safe area outside to look at spring plants and flowers or show them pictures or photographs of plants growing in a park or garden. Back inside, invite the children to create their own pop-up garden scene. Give each child two or more oval pieces of paper and some colouring materials. Encourage them to draw some colourful, enclosed shapes such as circles, ovals and irregular shapes on each sheet of paper to represent an array of simple flowers.

Invite the children to decorate inside the shapes using blocks of colour or patterns such as dots, random scribbles, spots, stripes and so on. When this is complete, give each child a sheet of green card with the pop-up sections. Help them to glue their imaginary flower pictures onto the two pop-up sections. Invite them to open and close the folded card to reveal their colourful pop-up garden scene.

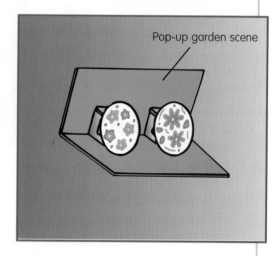

Pop-up garden scene

Let the children add extra details to the background, such as simple butterfly shapes, spiders, grass, ladybirds and so on. Some children may wish to copy or write a title for the picture along the bottom edge of their pop-up scene, for example, 'Katie's garden' or 'Spring flowers by Dari' and so on.

Support
Show the children how to draw a variety of enclosed shapes for them to copy, trace or use as a visual guide.

Extension
Invite the children to make 'raised pictures' to illustrate a garden scene by sticking textured materials onto the pop-up sections. Ideas could include flowers made from raised patterned wallpaper or tree trunks from corrugated card.

Daffodil button badges

What you need
Yellow and orange paint; painting materials; glue; spreaders; gold glitter; an assortment of yellow and orange paper shapes approximately 8cm x 6cm, such as triangles, ovals, hearts and irregular shapes; cardboard egg-box sections; a selection of beads in different shades of yellow and orange; thread; masking tape; aprons.

Preparation
Pierce a small hole in the base of each egg-box section.

What to do
Explain to the group the link between St David's Day and daffodils. Tell the children that they are going to make daffodil badges that they will be able to wear.

Help each child to paint the inside of an egg-box section in different shades of yellow or orange and leave to dry. Invite them to spread glue on the inside edges of their painted egg-box section and to sprinkle with gold glitter.

Ask each child to turn their egg-box section upside-down and to glue six or eight orange and yellow paper shapes around the outside, allowing the different shapes to overlap. Let the extra length of paper fan out over the table and leave to dry.

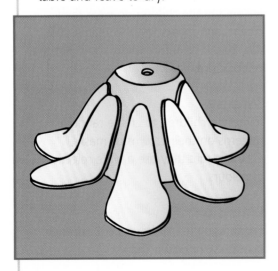

Invite each child to place three or four yellow or orange beads onto a length of thread and help them to pull the thread through the hole in the base of the decorated egg-box section, so that the beads sit snugly inside. Secure the thread at the back with masking tape to create a daffodil. Attach a loop of thread to the back of each daffodil to create a button badge.

Provide paper cups instead of egg-box sections and use the same technique to create large flowers for a display with a three-dimensional effect.

Encourage the children to use their imagination to add extra details to the flower display. These ideas could include green fabric cut into large leaf shapes, sponge-print butterflies folded in half to create wings that flap and so on.

Support
Provide the children with plenty of individual help during the gluing and threading stages.

Extension
Encourage the children to cut out their own paper shapes.

Crowns and masks

Learning objective
To use available resources to create props to support role-play.

Group size
Small groups.

What you need
For crowns: strips of colourful card approximately 10cm wide and long enough to fit around a child's head.
For face masks: discs of colourful card approximately 20cm diameter.
For eye masks: ovals of colourful card approximately 10cm x 20cm.
Shared resources: an assortment of decorative collage materials such as sequins, shiny paper, braid, lace, tissue, coloured paper, colourful 'flat' buttons and so on; strong glue; child-safe hole-punch; scissors; ribbon or wool; stapler (for adult use); an area suitable for imaginative role-play, aprons.

Preparation
Cut eye holes in the discs and ovals of card.

What to do
Talk with the children about the celebrations associated with 'Purim'. Invite each child to make a crown using a strip of card, a face mask using a disc of card, or an eye mask using an oval piece of card.

Provide a wide selection of decorative collage materials and glue and encourage the children to use their imagination to decorate their card shapes. Ideas could include repeated patterns using two or more colours; repeated patterns using two or more paper shapes; decorations in shades of one colour, for example, braid, sequins, glitter, shiny paper and so on in various shades of red; dangle designs, for example, gluing only the tip of braid or strips of paper to create a 'fringe effect'. When the children have decorated their shapes, leave these to dry.

Help the children to turn their strips of decorated card into crowns using a stapler, or the decorated discs and ovals into masks using a hole-punch and ribbon or wool to create 'ties'. Encourage the children to wear their crowns and masks for imaginative role-play based on information about Purim celebrations.

Support
Invite the children to create random patterns on their crowns or masks, ensuring that they use a wide selection of colours.

Extension
Encourage the children to cut out their own mask or crown shapes.

Home links
Ask parents and carers beforehand for contributions of braid, shiny materials, flat buttons and so on. Let the children take their crowns or masks home to inspire discussion about Purim with their families. Invite parents and carers who have firsthand experience of Purim festivals to talk to the children about the celebrations.

Happy hands

What you need
The photocopiable sheet on page 66; access to a laminator; red, blue, yellow and white paint; shallow trays large enough to fit a child's hand span; paintbrushes; aprons.

Preparation
Make an enlarged copy of the photocopiable sheet for each child.

What to do
Talk with the children about Mother's Day. Be sensitive to any individual circumstances and, if necessary, talk about a Special Person's Day.

Give each child a selection of paints in the primary colours (red, yellow and blue) and white. Invite them to mix two or more of the paints in a shallow tray to create a new shade or colour that they think their mother would enjoy.

Provide each child with an enlarged copy of the photocopiable sheet. Read the poem to the children and talk about the meaning. Next, encourage each child to use the paint colour that they have chosen to make a print of

each hand either side of the poem. When the prints are dry, help each child to write or copy their name, age and the name of their setting in the three boxes at the bottom of their 'Happy hands' sheet. Alternatively, scribe the words for them.

Laminate the sheets and invite each child to give their handprint to their special person as a keepsake.

Create a 'useful' keepsake by adding a notepad to the bottom edge of each laminated photocopiable sheet. Alternatively, add a list of your setting's holiday and event dates.

Use the poem to develop the children's poetic language. Encourage each child to tell you spontaneous words or phrases that describe their own mother (or special person).

Support
Help the children during the colour-mixing stage.

Extension
Invite the children to mix two new colours, one for each hand.

A colourful egg

What you need

A sheet of A1 thick white paper or thin card; plastic spoons; old toothbrushes; shallow trays; paints in complementary shades, for example, blue, lilac and purple, or red, orange and yellow; several strips of black paper approximately 10cm x 2cm; glue; display board at the children's own height; scissors; black backing paper; aprons; protective table covering; hard-boiled egg; pictures of real eggs, including eggs with mottled shells.

Preparation

Draw the outline of a giant egg shape onto a sheet of A1 white paper or card.

What to do

Talk to the children about why the shape of an egg is often seen during Easter time celebrations. Invite the children to handle the hard-boiled egg and talk about the size, shape and feel of the shell.

Show the children the pictures of eggs and encourage them to talk about the different shell colours. Invite them to work collectively to help decorate the 2-D giant egg shape.

Place the giant egg shape on a covered table. Give each child a tray of paint, an old toothbrush and a plastic spoon and invite them to dab the bristles of their toothbrushes into the paint. Show them how to scrape the plastic spoon across the top of the bristles to create a fine spray of paint across the giant egg. Continue this process several times using paints in complementary colours until the egg shape has a mottled appearance. Leave the egg to dry.

Next, help the children to glue several strips of narrow black paper

across the decorated egg in a zigzag design to create the appearance of an egg cracking, and leave this to dry.

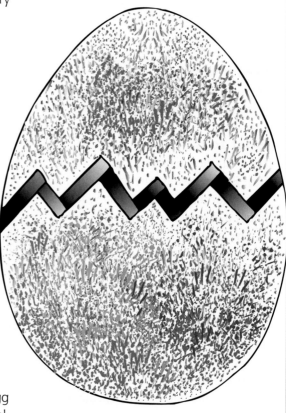

Cover a display board with black backing paper. Cut out the egg and mount it onto the display board.

Invite the children to write or copy Easter greetings onto strips of coloured paper. Encourage them to think of their own ideas.

Display the children's greetings around the giant egg on the display board for everyone to see and read.

Support

Provide the children with hand-over-hand support during the spraying stage.

Extension

Invite the children to help cut around the large egg and to cut out the black strips of paper.

Veggie colours

What you need
The photocopiable sheet on page 67; coloured pens, pencils or crayons; real cucumber, corn on the cob, potato and carrot; tray; role-play area; items to create an imaginary fruit and vegetable shop, for example, real or pretend fruit and vegetables, a table, a toy till, real or pretend money, baskets, carrier bags, weighing scales, notepad, pens, price labels, aprons, calculator and a sign saying 'Fruit and vegetable shop'; alternatively, a selection of items to create an imaginary vegetarian café, for example, tables, chairs, table-cloth, pretend candles, cups, plates, cutlery, menu, waiter/waitress outfits, toy till, real or pretend money, notepad and pens.

Preparation
Make a copy of the photocopiable sheet for each child.

What to do
Talk with the children about the significance of vegetables and vegetarian meals during Baisakhi. Place the assortment of raw vegetables on a tray and encourage the children to observe and touch each vegetable. Can the children identify them? Invite the group to talk about the different colours of each vegetable and which one they prefer.

Give each child a copy of the photocopiable sheet and encourage them to match each vegetable from your tray to the correct picture on their sheet. Then, ask them to colour in the vegetable pictures using the real vegetables as a colour guide.

When the pictures are complete, display them back to back as colourful mobiles in an area set up as a 'Fruit and vegetable shop' or a 'Vegetarian café'. Invite the children to use the role-play area for imaginative play, for example, buying and selling fruit and vegetables in the shop, or ordering and serving food in the café.

Support
Give the children an enlarged copy of the photocopiable sheet to allow for bold hand strokes.

Extension
Provide extra vegetables for the children to name and identify. Try to include a few vegetables that might be less familiar to them, such as sweet potato, aubergine, red onion, red cabbage and so on.

Learning objective
To choose particular colours to use for a purpose.

Group size
Individuals or small groups.

Home links
Ask parents and carers beforehand to donate a vegetable for the activity. Invite carers who have had firsthand experience of the Sikh New Year Festival to talk to the children about the celebrations and traditions.

Dragon body puppets

What you need
A large cardboard box for each child; finger-paints; sheets of A4 or A3 white card; cardboard egg-box sections; orange, red and blue tissue paper; glue; heavy-duty stapler (for adult use); wide parcel tape; two ribbons or narrow strips of fabric for each child approximately 45cm; aprons.

Preparation
Unseal the cardboard boxes, turn them inside out and reseal using a heavy-duty stapler and wide parcel tape to provide a blank surface free from logos. Remove the flaps except for one along the top edge and one along the bottom edge on the opposite side of each box.

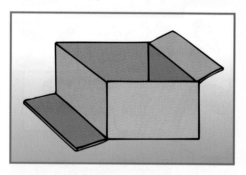

Staple a semi-oval of card to the top flap to represent a dragon's head, and a triangle of card to the bottom flap to represent a dragon's tail.

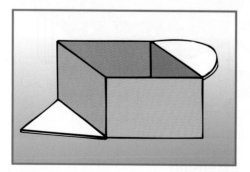

What to do
Talk to the children about the myths and legends associated with George and the Dragon and its relevance to St George's Day in England. Encourage the children to use their imagination to describe the appearance of a dragon, or to remember a drawing of a dragon that they may have seen in their story-books.

Give each child a prepared cardboard box. Explain that it represents a dragon's body, head and tail. Invite the children to decorate their dragons using your selection of finger-paints. Encourage each child to make an independent choice of colours, shapes, patterns, swirls or scribbles. Leave the boxes to dry.

Help each child to glue four egg-box sections onto each dragon's head – two to represent the dragon's eye sockets and two to represent the nostrils. Invite them to glue scrunched-up blue tissue into their dragon's eye sockets to show its eyes, and strips of red and orange tissue into the nostrils to represent flames. Then leave to dry.

Using ribbon or strips of fabric, help each child to tape two shoulder straps onto their box to create a dragon body puppet.

Encourage the children to wear their dragon body puppets to inspire imaginative play about 'George and the Dragon'.

Support
Invite the children to work in pairs to make a shared dragon body puppet.

Extension
Encourage the children to help during the preparation stages.

Floral patterns

What you need
The photocopiable sheet on page 68, paints; painting materials; small collage materials such as fabric, shiny paper, tissue paper, lentils, seeds, lace, braid and so on; drawing materials; glue; aprons; a wide selection of real flowers or pictures of flowers; display board at the children's height; table; floral cloth; baby doll.

Preparation
Make an enlarged copy of the photocopiable sheet for each child.

What to do
Talk to the children about why the theme of flowers is important during Hanamatsuri. Look at the real flowers or pictures of flowers with the children and talk about the different colours seen on the petals and within the centre of the flowers.

Invite the children to help create imaginary flowers for a colourful display. Give each child an enlarged copy of the photocopiable sheet and help them to cut around the outside edge. Ask them to decorate the flower on their sheet using a different media for each petal. For example, one petal could be painted, another could be covered in shiny paper, lace or lentils, another could be coloured using felt-tipped pens and so on. When the flowers are dry, encourage the children to help arrange them on a display board to represent the floral garden where the baby Buddha was born.

Invite the children to lay a baby doll, on a floral cloth beside the floral display to represent the baby Buddha lying in the garden.

Support
Help the children with cutting, gluing and keeping within the lines.

Extension
Provide a circular template and encourage the children to draw their own floral outline.

Mini maypoles

What you need
For each child: a dowelling rod approximately 30cm long; four coloured ribbons approximately 30cm long; a circular lid such as a cheese-triangles box lid.
Shared resources: pictures of maypole dancing; masking tape; coloured paper; scissors; glue.

Preparation
Cut a hole approximately 1cm–2cm in diameter in the centre of each circular cardboard lid.

What to do
Show the children your selection of pictures of maypole dancing and talk about the traditions and celebrations associated with May Day. Tell the group that you are going to make mini maypole spinning toys.

Give each child a circular cardboard lid (with a pre-cut hole), coloured paper, scissors and glue. Help them to decorate the surface of their lid by gluing on a collage of different paper shapes cut from their coloured paper. When this is dry, assist them with

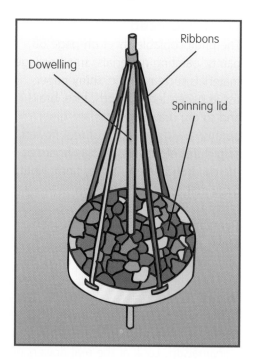

lid and to tape the four loose ends of ribbon to the top of the rod.

Invite each child to spin their decorated lid to create the effect of ribbons twisting around a maypole and let the group enjoy watching them go round and round.

Use the toys to inspire movement and dance on the theme of spinning, twisting and turning, or to reinforce traditional circle games such as 'Ring-a-ring-o-roses' and 'In and out the dusty bluebells'.

Support
Provide plenty of assistance to the children with cutting out their paper shapes. Give them hand-over-hand support when they are attaching the coloured ribbons to their decorated lids and dowelling rods.

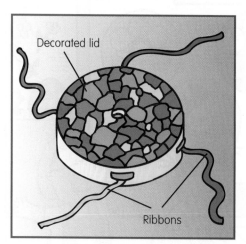

taping the four ribbons an equal distance apart around the outer rim of the decorated lid.

Help each child to place a dowelling rod through the hole in their decorated

Extension
Invite the children to reflect on the theme of spinning and twisting to help them make up short dance sequences with two or three repeated movements, for example, run, spin, jump, or skip, jump, spin.

Butterfly puppet

What you need

A safe area outside where butterflies can be seen; posters or picture books of butterflies; plain fabric; pots of coloured inks; absorbent paper such as kitchen roll; protective table covering; pinking shears (for adult use); long-arm stapler (for adult use); PVA glue; strips of stiff card approximately 3cm x 40cm; strips of black felt or card approximately 3cm x 20cm; water; pipettes (or clean brushes); aprons.

Preparation

For the butterfly wings: cut a simple fabric butterfly shape using pinking shears for each child.
For the butterfly body: trim the corners off a 20cm strip of black felt or card for each child.

What to do

Take the children on a supervised walk outside to observe butterflies in their natural habitat. Alternatively, look at pictures of butterflies in books or on posters. Talk with the children about the different colours and patterns that they can see on the butterfly wings.

Give each child some damp fabric butterfly wings and ask them to smooth out the wings across a sheet of absorbent paper. Invite them to use pipettes or clean brushes to drip coloured inks randomly over the butterfly wings.

Ask the children to observe the colours that spread and merge together. Talk about the new shades that emerge as one ink colour mixes with another.

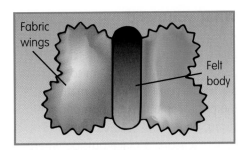

When the wings are dry. ask the children to glue a black felt butterfly body along the centre.

The children can then glue a long strip of stiff card to the underside of the butterfly to create a stick puppet.

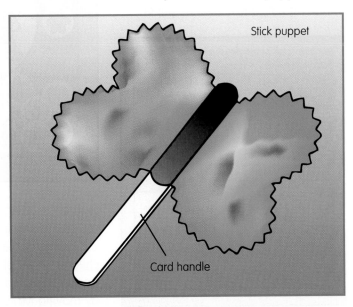

Stick puppet

Card handle

Alternatively, use a long-arm stapler to secure all three layers together, for example, the card, fabric and felt.

Encourage the children to use their puppets during imaginative play based on observations of real butterflies.

Support

Provide the children with only two coloured inks such as red and yellow or blue and red.

Extension

Encourage the children to make up simple butterfly stories during role-play and invite them to act them out to the rest of the group.

Learning objectives
To explore what happens when they mix colours; to engage in imaginative and role-play based on own firsthand experience.

Group size
Small groups.

Home links
Let the children take their butterfly stick puppets home. Invite them to bring in favourite picture books or stories based on butterflies or other minibeasts.

Story scenes

Learning objective
To begin to use representation as a means of communication.

Group size
Small or large groups.

What you need
A display board at the children's height; green backing paper; white circular paper approximately 10cm to 30cm in diameter; paints; painting materials; the photocopiable sheet on page 69; string; white oval card cut from A3 paper; scissors; a place outside where summer flowers can be seen or pictures of flowers; glue.

Preparation
Cover a display board with green backing paper and draw the outline of a winding pathway across the paper.

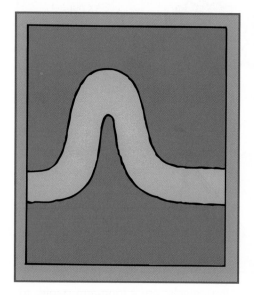

What to do
Read the story of 'Mr Goodman's garden' on the photocopiable sheet to the children and look at some flowers outside or at a selection of pictures of summer flowers.

Invite the children to help create a display showing Mr Goodman's garden in full bloom. Give each child one or more discs of paper and some paints, and invite the children to paint a colourful flower head to fill each disc. When this is dry, ask the children to glue the flower heads onto the display board, ensuring that they keep the pathway clear.

Invite a child to use their creative imagination to paint a picture of Mr Goodman on the oval card. When this is dry, tape a length of string to the top of the painting of Mr Goodman and

Mr Goodman can be moved along his garden

Children's flowers

secure the other end of the string to the top of the display.

Use the display to encourage the children to recall the story of 'Mr Goodman's garden' in their own words by moving Mr Goodman around the garden path.

Support
Let the children use large circular sponges to print flower shapes onto the discs of paper.

Extension
Invite the children to paint a selection of minibeasts to add to the display such, as ladybirds, butterflies and caterpillars.

Use the display to encourage mathematical vocabulary, for example, 'How many...?', 'Count the...', 'Are there more or less...?', 'Are there as many...?' and so on.

Home links
Ask parents and carers to accompany you on a walk with the children around a flower garden or park. Help the children to plant and care for easy-growing flowers to take home, such as sunflowers or nasturtiums.

Sunray dance

What you need
Strips of paper, fabric, crêpe paper, shiny paper and ribbon approximately 50cm by 3cm in 'sunshine' colours such as orange, cream and yellow; sticky tape; enough space to move around freely and safely; large PE hoops or circular mats.

What to do
Talk about the warmth of the sun and invite the children to discuss their favourite summer activities. Explain to the group that the sun is a very long way from us but we can feel the warmth of the rays coming out from it. Talk about the danger of sunrays and how we need to protect ourselves with suncream, sun-glasses and sun-hats.

Invite the children to make sunrays. Provide a wide selection of fabric and paper strips and ask each child to choose between five and ten strips. Help them to secure the strips together at one end using several pieces of sticky tape. Then invite the group to take their colourful sunray streamers into a safe, spacious area.

Encourage the children to pretend to be the sun by walking together in a large circle while waving their sunrays in the air. Then, ask them to move a little faster, for example, skipping or jogging. Next, help them to put a sequence of movements together, for example, walk, jump, skip, or jog, hop, walk. Remind them to move around the area in the same direction to avoid bumping into one another.

Finally, invite the children to make up an individual dance sequence using two or three repeated movements, for example, run, jump, run, jump, or skip, hop, jump, skip, hop, jump, while waving their sunray streamers.

Support
While the children are making their streamers, help them by holding their bundles of fabric and paper strips so that they can secure the ends together with tape.

Extension
Ask the children to work in pairs to create short 'Follow-my-leader' style dances.

Learning objectives
To use one object to represent another; to develop a repertoire of actions by putting a sequence of movements together.

Group size
Individuals or small groups.

Home links
Let the children take their streamers home. Encourage them to talk about their favourite summer pastimes while at home or out with their parents or carers.

T-shirt patch

What you need
The photocopiable sheet on page 70; fabric pen in a dark colour or permanent marker; fabric paints in orange and yellow; clean sponges; two shallow trays; pinking shears; white fabric; masking tape; absorbent paper such as kitchen roll; a clean T-shirt for each child; sharp scissors (for adult use); a sewing machine, or needle and thread (for adult use); aprons; access to a laminator (or clear, sticky-backed film).

Preparation
Make a copy of the photocopiable sheet for each child and laminate it or cover both sides with sticky-backed film. Cut around the lines to create a sun stencil. Using pinking shears, cut a square or disc of white fabric for each child approximately 20cm x 20cm. Place the fabric over some absorbent paper and use masking tape to secure the fabric onto a plastic tray or table top. Make sure that the fabric is taut.

What to do
Help each child to tape the sun stencil onto their fabric using short strips of masking tape.

Place a thin layer of yellow and orange fabric paint in separate trays. Invite each child to dab a sponge into the paint and then onto the fabric

Sun stencil   Masking tape

Taut fabric

through the holes in the stencil. Let them use one colour or a mixture of both orange and yellow.

When the fabric is dry, carefully remove the masking tape and stencils to reveal colourful sunshine prints. (The stencils can be reused). Invite the children to use a dark-coloured fabric pen or a permanent marker to draw a smiley face in the centre of the sun.

Sew the prints onto the front of each child's T-shirt. (Alternatively, the prints can be made directly on the T-shirts.)

Invite each child to reuse their stencil to create a smiley-face hand puppet by printing the sun design onto a paper bag. Alternatively, print it onto a rectangle of fabric. Glue or sew the fabric to fit a child's hand.

Support
To avoid damage to the stencils, demonstrate to the children how to dab the fabric gently with the sponge.

Extension
Invite the children to sign their names under their sun designs using a fabric pen or permanent marker.

Alternatively, encourage the children to draw and cut out their own stencil designs, helping them if necessary.

Our garden centre

What you need
To make flowers and plants: a wide variety of model-making materials, for example, cardboard tubes, boxes, pipe-cleaners, cotton reels, card, string, colourful paper, tissue, fabric, wool, seeds, lentils, tubs, lids, braid and beads; PVA glue; masking tape; sticky tape; aprons.

To make a garden centre: a role-play area; tables; price labels; toy till; real or pretend money; notepad; pen; bags; baskets; signs, for example, 'Pay here', 'Open', 'Closed', 'Plants for sale' and so on; plastic flowerpots.

Preparation
Arrange a garden centre in the role-play area.

What to do
Provide the children with a wide range of modelling materials and invite them to construct and decorate imaginative plants or flowers to display in the garden centre. Allow a high degree of independence. Ideas could include: gluing paper leaves onto the sides of a stalk to create an imaginary evergreen; gluing yellow fabric petals around a card lid and gluing seeds or lentils in the centre to create imaginary sunflower heads; and taping scrunched-up tissue paper onto green pipe-cleaners to create imaginary rosebuds. When the garden centre is complete, invite the children to use it to inspire imaginative play while buying and selling the plants and flowers.

Use the activity to introduce money, using real or pretend coins. Help the children to count out how much money is needed to buy something and to work out how much change to give.

Support
Invite the children to work in pairs to create a plant or flower.

Extension
Invite the children to write the price labels for the garden centre.

Learning objective
To make three-dimensional structures.

Group size
Small groups.

Home links
Invite parents and carers in to buy items from the garden centre. Ask them beforehand if they could save boxes, colourful paper, lids and so on for the children to make the flowers and plants.

Fragrant flowers

Learning objectives
To further explore an experience using a range of senses; to respond to comments and questions, entering into dialogue about their creations.

Group size
Small groups.

Home links
Let each child take a perfumed flower home. Ask parents and carers to help supervise a visit to a florist, or ask for contributions of real flowers to decorate the room and to show to the children.

What you need
A local florist or a selection of real flowers with a pleasant smell; a variety of fabric collage materials such as fabric swatches, felt, fur, lace, braid and wool; a display board at the children's height; green backing paper; glue; perfume sprays (for adult use); circular templates approximately 12cm in diameter; A3 paper or card; child-safe scissors.

Preparation
Cover the display board with green backing paper.

What to do
If possible, take the children on a supervised visit to a florist. Alternatively, show them a selection of some real fragrant flowers. Talk about the smell and appearance of the flowers and tell the children that they are going to make a display of collage flowers.

Give each child a sheet of A3 paper or card and ask them to draw around a circular template several times to create a floral shape on their sheet.

Invite the children to decorate their shapes using a range of fabric collage materials to create colourful and textured flowers. When this is complete, help each child to cut a circle around their flower design and to glue it randomly onto the display board.

Encourage each child to select their own favourite perfume spray. (NB Be aware of any allergies and make sure that perfumes are sprayed away from the child's face.) Help them to spray a little perfume onto their flower collage. When this is done, invite the children to talk about the appearance and smell of the display.

Support
Provide the children with fabric collage materials that you have pre-cut into small pieces.

Extension
Invite the children to draw their flower shapes freehand.

Lovely lanterns

What you need
A strip of black sugar paper approximately 20cm x 65cm for each child; coloured tissue paper approximately 10cm x 10cm; coloured shiny sequins or snippets of coloured shiny paper; glue stick; gold and silver pens (optional); coloured ribbon or strips of coloured paper 30cm long.

Preparation
Fold each sheet of black paper four times at regular intervals: 15cm, 30cm, 45cm and 60cm.

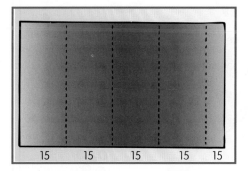

What to do
Talk to the children about the Buddhist festival of Wesak. Explain that as part of the traditions, homes are decorated with lanterns.

Invite the children to make colourful lanterns to decorate the room. Give each child a sheet of black sugar paper showing four fold lines. Help them to cut a simple shape across each of the three main folds to create three decorative holes.

Help the children to glue coloured tissue paper over the back of each hole. Then invite each child to decorate the front of their black paper using coloured sequins or coloured snippets of shiny paper.

Help each child to refold their decorated sheet of black paper and then to glue along the flap to create an open-ended box shape representing a lantern.

Finally, invite each child to tape a length of coloured ribbon or strip of coloured paper across the top of their lantern to create a handle.

Hang the lanterns at low level around the room to provide an interesting and colourful display.

Support
Provide the children with hand-over-hand help during the gluing and refolding stages.

Extension
Invite the children to help with the preparation and to plan their designs by discussing colours, shapes and patterns for their lanterns.

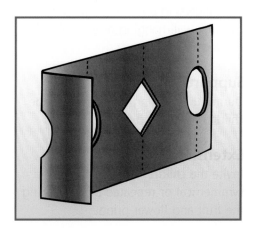

Learning objective
To make three-dimensional structures.

Group size
Individuals or small groups.

Home links
Invite the children to take their lanterns home to decorate their bedrooms.

Ask parents and carers who have had firsthand experience of Wesak celebrations to talk to the children and to show them real, traditional lanterns that they have used to decorate their homes.

Fruit and flowers

What you need

A selection of fruit, some suitable for printing such as apples and pears; knife (for adult use); plastic trays or plates; fabric or poster paints; plain cotton fabric approximately 1m x 1m; masking tape; protective table covering; absorbent paper such as kitchen roll; circular objects suitable for printing such as corks, round sponges, cotton reels, plastic bottle lids and so on.

Preparation

Place the fabric on a table over a protective covering and absorbent paper. Secure it around the edges with masking tape to keep it taut.

What to do

Talk with the children about the Jewish festival of Shavuot. Explain that during these celebrations, Jewish people decorate synagogues with fruit and flowers. Invite the children to help make fruit and flower prints to decorate the room.

Provide a range of fruit for the children to handle and to feel its texture. Slice the fruit and let the children observe the shapes and patterns inside each fruit. Encourage them to talk about the different smells, telling you which one they prefer.

Next, let the children put apple and pear halves into a tray containing a thin layer of fabric paint (or poster paint) and then press them onto the taut

fabric. Invite the children to repeat the process several times, using different colours. Provide a range of circular printing objects such as corks, cotton

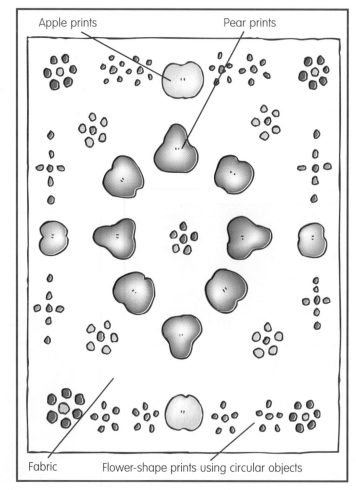

Apple prints   Pear prints

Fabric   Flower-shape prints using circular objects

reels and sponges and invite the children to use them to print flower shapes onto the fabric.

When the printed fabric is dry, help the children to use it to create a floor cushion, wall hanging or a simple window blind.

Support

During the printing stage, provide the children with hand-over-hand help.

Extension

Invite the children to create symmetrical or repeated patterns using the fruit and flower prints.

Fabric flags

What you need
Triangles of plain fabric approximately 20 to 30cm long, cut using pinking shears to prevent fraying; a selection of coloured inks; plastic tubs such as small margarine tubs; large tray; masking tape; small, clean paintbrushes; absorbent paper such as kitchen roll; ribbon or narrow strips of non-fraying fabric; fabric glue; aprons.

What to do
Talk with the children about Midsummer's Day. Explain that many traditions still exist including bonfires, feasts and torchlit processions but the most common celebration is the summer fair.

Invite the children to help create a colourful, lively display of summer fair flags. Make sure that the children are wearing aprons. Give each child a triangle of fabric placed on several layers of absorbent paper. Secure several plastic tubs onto a tray using masking tape to prevent them from tipping over. Place a different-coloured ink into each pot with its own clean paintbrush.

Invite the children to paint the ink onto their fabric triangles. Explain to them that the colours will spread so they can create unusual flowing patterns. When the colours mix together, new shades will emerge. Leave the fabric flags to dry. Encourage

the children to use fabric glue to secure several 'flags' along a length of coloured ribbon. Hang the strip of flags across a display board showing the children's summer fair pictures and paintings.

Alternatively, organize a real summer fair and use the flags to decorate the entrance of your setting. Help the children to mix poster paints to create colourful banners and signs, for example, 'Welcome to our fair', 'Cake stall', or 'Have a great time'.

Support
Provide the children with only two coloured inks, such as red and yellow, so that they can see a third colour clearly emerge and recognize it.

Extension
Encourage the children to cut out their fabric shapes themselves.

Alternatively, invite them to use inks in the primary colours (red, yellow and blue) to create secondary colours such as orange, green and purple. Can they name these colours?

Learning objective
To use ideas involving fitting and overlapping.

Group size
Individuals and small groups.

Someone special

What you need
A disc of paper approximately 15cm in diameter for each child; the photocopiable sheet on page 71; blue and green marbling inks; tray; water; protective mat; aprons; scissors; paper fasteners; glue.

Preparation
Follow the instructions provided with the marbling inks. Make a copy of the photocopiable sheet onto card for each child.

What to do
Talk with the children about Father's Day. Be sensitive to any individual circumstances and, if necessary, talk about a Special Person's Day. Invite each child to make a card with moving parts to send to someone that they think is special.

Give each child a disc of paper and ask them to carefully dip it into the blue and green marbling inks. While the prints are drying, provide each child with a card copy of the photocopiable sheet. Ask them to cut carefully around the outside line of the circle. Invite them to draw a picture of their special person on the spinner arm and to cut it out.

Next, help each child to glue their marble print within the circle on the photocopiable sheet. Explain that this represents the world. Pierce a hole in each spinner arm and a hole in the centre of each 'world' for the children. Then, help each child to attach the spinner arm to the 'world' using a paper fastener. Invite them to spin the

The best in the world

Spinner arm

Photocopiable sheet

Blue/green marble print

picture of their special person around the wording 'The best in the world'.

Support
Cut out the disc and the spinner arm on the photocopiable sheet for the children.

Alternatively, provide an enlarged copy of the photocopiable sheet so it is easier for the children to handle.

Extension
Invite each child to write independently a message to their special person on the back of their card.

Alternatively, encourage the children to use ideas involving fitting and overlapping to design their own 'best in the world' cards. Suggestions could include a pop-up card showing a special person emerging from behind a globe, or a giant-sized card decorated in an array of colourful collage materials.

Home links
Let the children take their cards home. Organize an 'open day' so that the children can invite relatives and other special people into your setting.

✧ Come for a ride!

What you need

Two or three large, deep cardboard boxes; two large, shallow cardboard boxes; string; protective mat or newspaper; thick paint in two contrasting colours such as red and yellow; thick and thin paintbrushes; large paint containers; selection of coloured paints; large blue drape or old sheet; aprons.

Preparation

Link four or five large cardboard boxes together using string and trim the sides of the centre boxes.

What to do

Tell the children the traditional story associated with the Dragon Boat Festival. Show them the linked boxes that you have prepared and invite them to help one another to decorate the boxes to create a model dragon boat for imaginative play.

Place the boxes on a protective mat or newspaper. Invite the children to paint them using red paint and large paintbrushes. When the boxes are dry, encourage the children to decorate them with lines, patterns, swirls and shapes using yellow paint and thin paintbrushes.

Invite the children to choose a selection of colours to paint a dragon's

face on the front of their model boat, then leave it to dry. Place the finished dragon boat on a long strip of blue fabric to represent water. Encourage the children to use the model for imaginative play.

Alternatively, provide a selection of colourful fabrics, netting or drapes for the children to dress up as a Chinese dragon and to re-create a special parade or carnival procession. Play authentic music to create a carnival atmosphere.

Follow up the activity by inviting the children to create a small version of the 'dragon boat' for use with toys or teddies, or during imaginative play.

Support

To avoid this activity becoming messy, invite the children to take turns at painting small areas of the model with one to one adult supervision.

Extension

Invite the children to cut out decorative shapes and details from large sheets of coloured card to add to their model, for example, a dragon's tail, teeth, tongue, flames and so on.

Raindrops keep falling

What you need
A display board at the children's height; blue backing paper; foil or shiny paper in shades of silver and blue; textured collage materials such as wool, colourful fabric swatches, braid, tissue, card, paper and so on; scissors; glue; thick black marker pen; sticky tape; fine thread in white, blue or silver; A2 or A3 sheets of thick paper; a selection of musical instruments suitable to imitate rain and thunder.

Preparation
Cover a display board with blue backing paper. Use a thick marker pen to draw a simple, bold outline of an

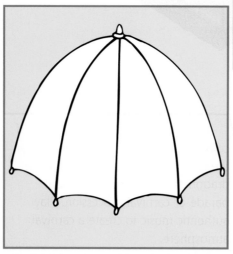

umbrella, without a handle, onto three or more large sheets of paper.

What to do
Talk to the children about St Swithun's Day. Invite them to decorate the prepared umbrella outlines with colourful, textured collage materials. As the children work, encourage them to talk about the different colours and textures that they are using. When the umbrella shapes are complete, secure them along the bottom edge of the display board.

Next, invite the children to cut out small shapes from silver foil or shiny

paper to represent raindrops. Ask the children to glue some of the raindrops randomly over the display. Help them to tape varying lengths of fine thread to the other raindrops and hang them

Hanging raindrops

Umbrella collages   Glued raindrops

along the top edge of the display board to provide a 3-D effect.

Ask the children to sit in a circle around the display board, and use the display to inspire singing songs and rhymes about rain, such as 'Dr Foster', 'Rain, Rain Go Away', 'I'm Singing in the Rain' and so on.

Finally, provide the children with some musical instruments to make the sound of rain and thunderstorms. For example, triangles tapped gently can sound like rain, whilst triangles, drums and shakers played loudly together can sound like thunder.

Support
Help the children to cut out the raindrop shapes.

Extension
Encourage the children to write colour words such as 'red' or 'blue' in the different sections on each umbrella, and ask them to use collage materials to match each colour word.

Beads and bracelets

What you need

Air-drying clay; clay mat or board; blunt matchsticks; small pieces of old fabric approximately 10cm x 10cm; poster paints; varnish (optional); various threads such as thin ribbon, cord and thick wool; aprons; role-play area.

What to do

Talk to the children about the Hindu festival of Raksha Bandhan and invite each child to make and decorate a bead for the centre of a rakhi (a thread bracelet) to give to a special friend.

Provide each child with a small ball of clay the size of a walnut or cherry tomato, and ask them to place the ball of clay onto a small piece of fabric in the centre of a clay board or mat. Encourage them to press the ball of clay with the palm of their hand until it is flat. Next, help them to poke two small holes in the middle of their clay shape using a blank matchstick so that it resembles a large button. Leave each clay shape to dry on the small pieces of fabric. Then invite the children to remove the fabric and to paint and varnish their clay shapes to create large colourful beads.

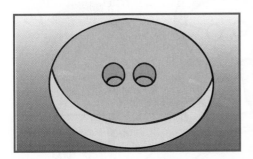

Help each child to thread their bead onto coloured ribbon or wool to create a rakhi for a friend.

Encourage the children to use their rakhis during role-play based on the story of Raksha Bandhan.

Create an interactive display about the festival of Raksha Bandhan. Include books and pictures or photographs of the celebration, examples of traditional rakhis and a collection of materials used to create rakhis.

Invite a parent, carer or grandparent to come in to talk about their life as a child in another country or another town or village. Help the children to understand that children growing up all over the world have a lot in common, such as making and playing with new friends and learning new skills.

Support

Provide plenty of assistance to the children with pressing the balls of clay and making them flat.

Extension

Invite the children to paint their beads using spots, stripes or patterns.

Alternatively, let the children make and paint spherical beads with a single hole through the centre.

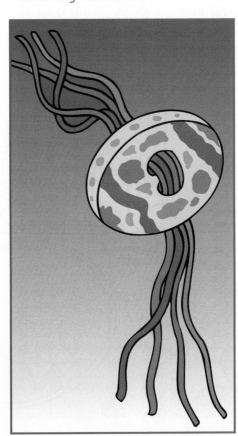

Learning objectives
To work creatively on a small scale; to introduce a story line or narrative into their play.

Group size
Pairs or small groups.

Home links
Let the children take their rakhis home to give to a brother, friend or soft toy.

Midnight stars

What you need
The photocopiable sheet on page 72;
gold and silver pens or pencils; glue;
glitter; snippets of shiny paper; scissors;
shiny thread or ribbon; sticky tape;
large PE hoop; musical instruments;
tape recorder.

Preparation
Make a copy of the photocopiable
sheet for each child.

What to do
Talk with the children about the Hindu
festival which celebrates Krishna's birth.
Give each child a copy of the
photocopiable sheet and invite them to
decorate the star using gold and silver
pens or crayons. Ask them to carefully
cut around the outside lines of the star
shape and then to decorate the reverse
side of the star using glue and glitter or
snippets of shiny paper.

Alternatively, provide each child with
more than one photocopiable sheet to
decorate, for example, a reduced or
enlarged sheet, or provide stars of

varying sizes. Help the children to tape
their stars to a large PE hoop using
varying lengths of shiny thread or
ribbon. Hang the hoop (or hoops) so
that the stars are just out of reach. Use
the mobile to reinforce favourite songs
and rhymes about stars or night-time,
for example, 'Twinkle, Twinkle, Little
Star' and 'Wee Willie Winkie', or to
inspire the children to make up their
own songs about stars or night-time.

Provide a selection of musical
instruments and a tape recorder for
the children to experiment recording
sounds and songs on their own or
within a group. Listen to the 'new'
music together. Invite the children to
say what they like about the recordings.

Support
Assist the children with cutting out their
star shapes.

Extension
Use the photocopiable sheet to make
a card template for the children to
draw around.

Autumn changes

What you need
The photocopiable sheet on page 73; paints; painting materials; paper; aprons; display board; fallen but clean autumn leaves.

Preparation
Make an enlarged copy of the poem on the photocopiable sheet.

What to do
Read the poem 'Autumn changes' to the children. Explain that the poem describes the changes that occur in autumn. Have the children noticed any of the changes that are mentioned in the poem?

Provide each child with paints, paper and painting equipment and invite them to paint a picture to illustrate one of the animals or plants mentioned in the poem, for example, squirrels, hedgehogs, coloured leaves, fir cones, conkers and so on.

Display the paintings on the wall around an enlarged copy of the poem and decorate them further with the clean autumn leaves, scattering them among the pictures and poem.

Use the display to inspire discussion by encouraging the children to talk about their own experiences or memories of autumn. Invite each child to paint a 'freestyle' picture about their experience or memory. Hang the paintings near to the display or use them to create a pictorial big book.

Encourage the children to paint a 'freestyle' picture about each of the other seasons, and collate the pictures to create three more big books to provide an 'Around the year' compilation that the children can go back to during the year.

Support
Draw simple, bold outlines for the children to decorate with paint.

Extension
Encourage the children to write or copy the text from the poem which they chose to illustrate.

Learning objective
To try to capture experiences and responses with paint.

Group size
Small groups.

Home links
Invite parents and carers to take their children for an autumn walk to collect interesting items for a 'look and touch' display. Ask them to encourage their children to paint or draw an autumn picture at home to include in the display.

Fingerprint trees

What you need
A safe area outside to look at autumn trees and leaves; A4 sheets of paper or card; A4 card frames; black or dark brown ink or runny paint; four shallow trays containing yellow, orange, red and brown paint; plastic straws; pipettes or thick paintbrushes; glue; aprons; display board.

Preparation
Glue an A4 card frame onto an A4 sheet of paper or card for each child. This helps to contain the paint.

What to do
Take the children outside to look at autumn trees. Observe the sturdy trunks, the bare branches and the tangles of fine branches.
Back inside, invite the children to use two different painting techniques to create autumn tree pictures. Give each child a sheet of framed card and invite them to paint a simple black tree trunk half-way down the centre of the card.
Next, using a pipette or thick paintbrush, help each child to drop a small amount of black ink or runny paint at the top of the tree trunk. Then invite them to use a plastic straw to blow the paint outwards and upwards to create the appearance of tangled branches. Ask them to repeat this process, until the top half of the card is full of branches.
When the paint is dry, invite the children to dip their fingertips into a shallow tray of yellow paint to print a random pattern over the tree and its 'branches' to represent yellow leaves. Next, help the children to repeat the fingertip prints using orange, red and brown paint respectively, and leave the tree shapes to dry.
Finally, hang the pictures on a display board to create an exhibition of 'Autumn trees'.

Support
Show the children how to hold and move the straw very close to the paper while blowing.

Extension
Invite the children to help you with the preparation stages by cutting and gluing the card frames onto the sheets of A4 paper or card.

Simple tree trunk painting

Red, orange, yellow, fingertip prints

Brown or black ink or paint blown across card

Hiding hedgehog

What you need
Books showing pictures of hedgehogs; fallen but clean autumn leaves; PVA glue; sheet of brown A2 paper; pencil; brown crayons; one large and one small black button or discs of black sticky paper; a prickly brush or comb; brown felt.

Preparation
Draw a simple, bold outline of a hedgehog on a sheet of brown A2 paper.

What to do
Show the children some pictures of hedgehogs. Ask them if they have ever seen a real hedgehog. Talk about what a hedgehog looks like. Can the children imagine what a hedgehog would feel like if they could touch one? Invite them to gently feel a prickly comb or brush that is similar to a hedgehog's spiky body. Encourage the children to describe the texture of the brush or comb as they touch it.

Explain that hedgehogs sleep during the winter months when their food of beetles, slugs, caterpillars and snails is hard to find, and that they wake up when it gets warmer and more food is available. Introduce the word 'hibernation' to the children and explain to them that you would like to create together a picture of a hedgehog hidden in its winter nest.

Show the children the hedgehog outline that you have prepared and encourage them to colour the hedgehog's face using shades of brown, add two black buttons (or sticky paper) for an eye and nose and a semicircle of felt for an ear. Ask the children to cover the hedgehog's body in autumn leaves to give it a cosy nest.

Display the textured picture within easy reach of the children. Use the display to encourage discussion about different textures, for example, 'crunchy' leaves, a 'shiny' nose and a 'smooth' ear.

Follow up the activity by inviting the children to look for objects or artefacts in the room or outside your setting, which have different textures. Encourage the children to describe each texture by placing items in a 'feely' box and play a guessing game.

Support
Encourage the children to feel, compare and describe a variety of textures around the room.

Extension
Introduce the word 'hibernaculum' (a special nest of leaves) to the children to describe the hedgehog's winter nest.

Learning objective
To begin to describe the texture of things.

Group size
Small groups.

Home links
Invite parents and carers to explore different textures with their children using appropriate vocabulary such as 'soft', 'spiky', 'hard' and so on. Encourage them to provide paper, small scraps of different-textured materials and glue for their children to create collages at home.

Autumn colours

Learning objective
To choose particular colours to use for a purpose.

Group size
Individuals or small groups.

What you need
The photocopiable sheet on page 74; paper; glue; scissors; coloured pencils; writing pencils; small booklet for each child; a safe place outside with an abundance of autumn leaves.

Preparation
Make a copy of the photocopiable sheet for each child. Fold three pieces of A4 paper and staple them together to make the booklets. Write 'Autumn colours' and each child's name on the front.

What to do
Take the children on an autumn walk to look at a variety of different-coloured leaves. Back inside, give each child a copy of the photocopiable sheet, showing the outlines of four autumn leaves. Talk with the children about the colours that they could use for each leaf, such as orange, brown, yellow, red and green. Invite each child to select four different autumn colours, one for

each leaf. Ask them to cut out the first leaf and to stick it on the inside page of their booklet. Scribe some words relating to the colour of the leaf underneath the picture, for example, 'A green leaf' or 'A red leaf'. On the facing page, ask them to draw a picture of something in a matching colour. Scribe the picture description for them, for example, 'A green ball' or 'A red hat'. Repeat the process for each of the coloured leaves.

Invite the children to draw and colour their own leaves and pictures on the last two pages. Ask the children to place their picture booklets in the book corner to share with their peers.

Support
Help the children to cut out the leaves and stick them in the booklet.

Extension
Invite the children to write or copy the words in their booklet.

Home links
Ask parents and carers if they could help to supervise an autumn walk. Encourage them to help their children use real leaves and trays of paint to make autumn leaf prints at home.

Textured tiles

What you need
A safe place outside to collect natural autumnal materials such as sycamore seeds, acorns, beech nuts, acorn cups and so on; deep lids such as coffee jar lids; interior filler; aprons; blunt pencils; varnish.

Preparation
Mix the filler according to the instructions on the packet and pour a small amount into a lid for each child, approximately 2cm to 3cm deep.

What to do
Take the children outside to collect a selection of natural autumnal materials. Back inside, let the children dry, sort and compare their items, then invite them to talk about their shapes, textures and sizes. Encourage descriptive language and comparisons, for example, 'smooth', 'rough', 'bumpy', 'light brown', 'reddish brown', 'shiny', 'dull' and so on.

Give each child a lid containing the filler. Invite them to gently press a selection of the natural materials into the filler to create an autumn pattern of their choice. Encourage them to work until their pattern is complete as the filler will gradually set!

When the children have finished their patterns, invite each child to poke a hole in the top of their filler using a blunt pencil. When the filler has set, help them to remove it from the mould, and leave it to dry. Assist the children with the varnishing of their textured tiles and when these are dry, let each child thread a ribbon through the hole for hanging.

Follow up the activity by taking the children outside to find and feel natural objects of a contrasting texture, for example, soft grasses, evergreen leaves, moss, lichen and so on. Ask the children why the original collection of objects was more suitable for creating a textured tile.

Support
Make sure that the children do not bury the natural materials by pressing them too hard into the filler.

Extension
Invite the children to wear gloves and aprons to help prepare the filler. (NB Check for any skin allergies.)

Learning objectives
To show an interest in what they see, touch and feel; to make comparisons.

Group size
Individuals or small groups.

Home links
Let each child take their textured tile home as an unusual gift for a friend or relative. Encourage parents and carers to help their children to use moulding powder for making plaster castings at home.

Sounds of autumn

Learning objective
To explore the different sounds of instruments.

Group size
Small or large groups.

What you need

A variety of musical instruments; a selection of everyday objects which can be used to make sounds such as a biscuit tin, spoons, crunchy paper, hollow box, a ridged plastic bottle with a pencil 'scraper', blocks of wood and so on.

What to do

Choose a wet and windy day to carry out this activity and talk with the children about the sounds that they can hear outside, for example, rain dripping, wind howling, leaves scattering and so on.

Ask the children to sit in a circle and give each child a musical instrument or one of the everyday objects. Encourage them to take turns to make a sound using their instruments or objects. Compare the sounds to those that they can hear outside.

Encourage the children to have fun experimenting with their musical instruments and objects to create different sounds, for example, quiet sounds that depict the pitter-patter of raindrops or a gentle breeze, followed by loud, crashing sounds to depict a heavy thunderstorm.

Sing the song, 'I Hear Thunder' with the children.

I hear thunder, I hear thunder;
Hark, don't you, Hark don't you?
Pitter-patter raindrops,
Pitter-patter raindrops,
I'm wet through,
SO ARE YOU!

I see blue skies, I see blue skies
Way up high, way up high;
Hurry up the sunshine,
Hurry up the sunshine
We'll soon dry,
We'll soon dry!

Encourage the children to adapt the sounds that they make with their instruments or objects to match the words in the song. Ask them to swap instruments or objects around and repeat the activity.

Support

Ask the children to think of other weather songs or rhymes that they could play their instruments to.

Extension

Invite the children to make and decorate their own musical instruments from an assortment of reusable materials, for example, yoghurt-pot shakers, tin drums and so on.

Home links
Ask parents and carers to bring in a collection of wet-weather gear for their children such as wellington boots, waterproof coat, umbrella, hat and so on. Ask for the carers' permission to take the children outside to play in the rain if it is not too cold.

A wonderful world

Learning objective
To respond to comments and questions, entering into dialogue about their creations.

Group size
Small groups

What you need
Discs of white paper approximately 30cm in diameter; colourful magazines with a wide variety of pictures showing positive aspects of the world such as people at work and play, places, animals, homes, seas, land, rivers, weather, plants, flowers, children, babies and so on; scissors; glue; thread.

Preparation
Cut out a variety of pictures from the magazines.

What to do
Talk with the children about the celebrations associated with the Jewish festival of Rosh Hashana and explain to them that it celebrates the creation of the world.

Provide each child with a disc of paper and say that it represents the world. Invite the children to look through the collection of pictures that you have cut from magazines showing life on earth. Encourage each child to select several pictures which make them feel happy and which show a 'wonderful world'. Invite them to use glue to stick their selection of pictures onto their disc of paper.

Hang the 'worlds' back to back at the children's eye level to create a thought-provoking display. Use the display to inspire discussion about the pictures. For example, ask the children questions such as 'Where is your favourite place'?, 'What is your favourite game?', 'Who are your best friends?', 'What can you tell me about your "wonderful world" picture?' and so on.

Support
Encourage the children to ask questions or to talk about the pictures as they sort and glue them.

Extension
Provide the children with scissors and magazines. Invite each child to choose the pictures that they like and then to make their own picture collection to choose from for their 'world'.

A photo for you

What you need
The photocopiable sheet on page 75; A4 card; thread; sticky tape; glue; scissors; colourful finger-paints; aprons; a photograph of each child brought from home.

Preparation
Make a copy of the photocopiable sheet onto A4 card for each child. Ask parents and carers if the children can bring in recent photographs of themselves

What to do
Talk to the children about their grandparents and how special they are. Be sensitive to any individual circumstances and, if necessary, talk about a Special Person's Day.

Invite the children to make photo frames as gifts for their grandparents or special people. Give each child a copy of the photocopiable sheet and a selection of colourful finger-paints. Start by reading the words that are on the sheet to the children. Then ask each child to select some finger-paints in their favourite colours to make fingerprints and thumb-prints in the appropriate circles around the frame on their photocopiable sheet. When the paint is dry, invite them to stick their photograph in the centre of their frame. Help them to tape a loop of thread to the back of the frame so that it can be hung on the wall.

Arrange an exhibition of the children's photo frames on a display board at the children's eye level for everyone to see.

Support
Help the children during the finger- and thumb-printing stage.

Extension
Let the children use cameras to take photographs of one another to stick in their frames.

Citrus colours

What you need
A selection of different-coloured citrus fruit such as oranges, lemons and limes; a selection of thick paints in citrus shades such as orange, yellow and lime-green; printing materials; squares of white paper approximately 30cm x 30cm; squares of black paper approximately 30cm x 30cm; aprons; display board.

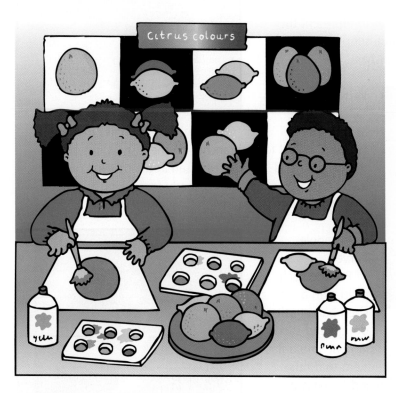

What to do
Talk with the children about the Jewish festival of Sukkot. Explain to them that it celebrates fruit harvest, especially citrus fruit.

Show the children some real citrus fruit and talk about the different colours. Give each child a selection of thick paints in citrus shades and a large square of white paper. Invite them to paint bold lines, patterns or fruit shapes. While the paint is still wet, help each child to carefully press a square of black paper on top of their painting. After a few seconds, assist them with carefully peeling the black paper away

from the white paper to reveal a 'printed' copy of their citrus painting.

Create a vibrant display by mounting the black and white pictures across a display board in a 'chessboard' design. Use the display to inspire discussion about colours, colour names and favourite colours.

Alternatively, invite the children to use the fruit, cut in half, to create colourful prints along narrow strips of black and white paper. When the printed strips are dry, use them to create an unusual border around the children's observational paintings of citrus fruit.

Follow up the activity by encouraging the children to help you make a colourful fruit salad. If possible, include fruit which may be less familiar to the children, such as sharon fruit, star fruit, kiwi fruit or passion fruit. (NB Emphasize the need for hygiene and hand washing before and during the activity.)

Support
Assist the children by giving them hand-over-hand support during the 'printing' stage.

Extension
Provide the children with a variety of paints and invite them to mix their own 'citrus' shades.

Learning objectives
To begin to differentiate colours; to differentiate marks and movements on paper.

Group size
Small groups.

Home links
Invite the children to make mini citrus prints using small sheets of paper and to take them home. Ask parents and carers for contributions to a fruit display to include some of the more unusual or exotic fruit such as star fruit, pineapple, kumquats, sharon fruit and so on.

Apple harvest

What you need
Salt dough; modelling board or mat; brown non-fraying fabric strips approximately 2cm x 6cm; red and green poster paints; varnish; display board; backing paper in shades of blue, light green and brown; rolling-pin (optional); stapler; aprons.

Preparation
Cover a display board in blue and green backing paper to represent the sky and grass. Add a simplistic brown tree trunk and branches.

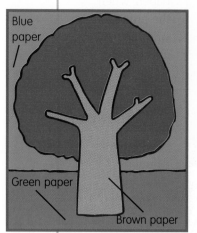

Blue paper

Green paper

Brown paper

What to do
Talk about the meaning of Harvest Festival to the children and invite them to create a display based on an apple harvest.

Provide each child with a fist-sized ball of salt dough and show them how to roll (or pat) one into a flat circular shape. Invite them to do the same with their own and to make a small hole at the edge with their finger.

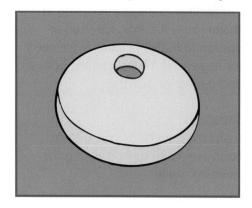

When the salt dough is dry, invite each child to paint their flat disc using red and/or green poster paints to represent a ripe apple. When the paint is dry, assist them with the varnishing of their apple and then leave the varnish to dry.

Provide each child with a strip of brown fabric and ask them to thread it through the hole in their apple, to represent a stalk.

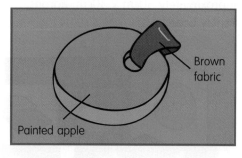

Brown fabric

Painted apple

Staple the apple stalks to the tree branches on the display board to represent an apple tree full of juicy apples, ready for picking at Harvest time!

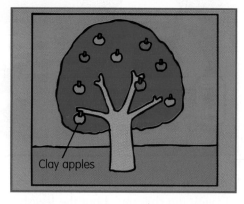

Clay apples

Support
Provide individual help to the children when they are making the hole in their apple so that it is made in the correct place.

Extension
Use the display to inspire mathematical language, for example, 'How many red apples are there on the tree?', 'How many apples are there altogether?', 'Are there more green or red apples?', 'If you could add one more apple, how many would there be altogether?' and so on.

Divali garlands

What you need
For the activity: string; coloured materials suitable for threading such as beads, cut-up straws and coloured pasta tubes; small discs of coloured netting or tissue paper.
For role-play: dressing-up box; decorations; pretend food; paper plates and cups.

What to do
Talk with the children about the Hindu festival of Divali. Explain to them that during the celebrations, colourful garlands are often offered to family and friends.

Invite the children to make colourful garlands by threading an assortment of beads, pasta and cut-up straws in between discs of coloured netting or

decorative fabrics and clothing and letting the group use them freely.

Invite the children to make paper chains and other colourful decorations for the home corner.

Provide paper cups and plates for the children to decorate, as well as pretend food. Let the group use the objects during role-play based on a festive meal.

Focus on other traditions associated with Divali. For example, help the children to make clay diva lamps and then decorate them with brightly coloured paint, and invite them to make pretend candles for the divas using small plastic lids and twists of tissue paper to represent the flames.

Alternatively, invite the children to create rangoli patterns using natural materials such as flower petals, rice, flour and coloured spices. Explain that rangoli patterns are usually symmetrical and are drawn on doorsteps during the festival of Divali.

Invite parents, carers and/or grandparents who celebrate Divali to show the children henna patterns which are traditionally drawn in the hands during the festival.

Support
Encourage the children to think about the colours and patterns on their garlands before they start painting.

Extension
Encourage the children to create garlands using a repeated pattern of colours, shapes or materials.

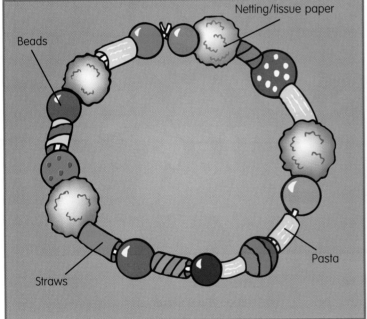
Netting/tissue paper
Beads
Straws
Pasta

tissue paper. When this is complete, help the children to tie the two ends of string together so that the garlands fit safely and easily over their heads. Invite them to wear their garlands during imaginative play about special days or party time.

Set the scene for imaginative play by providing a dressing-up box containing

Learning objectives
To make a construction; to pretend that one object represents another especially when objects have characteristics in common.

Group size
Small groups.

Home links
Invite the children to wear their garlands at home time.

Encourage parents and carers to provide a small quantity of beads, dried pasta or cut-up straws for their children to make garlands at home for toys or teddies.

Whizz, bang, whoosh!

What you need
A variety of percussion instruments such as triangles, drums, tambours, tambourines and so on; a room with enough space to move freely and safely; picture of firework (optional).

What to do
Discuss with the children their memories and experiences of Bonfire Night. Talk about the colours and sounds of fireworks. Invite the children to recreate some of the sounds using made-up words or noises such as 'Whizz', 'Bang', 'Whoosh' and so on.

Ask half of the group to sit in a large circle or around the edges of the room, and give each child a percussion instrument. Invite the rest of the children to crouch down on the floor in the centre of the circle (or room).

Encourage the children with the instruments to make a noise, all at the same time, to represent a burst of fireworks going off into the sky. Tell the children who are crouching on the floor to listen to the sounds and to pretend to be the exploding fireworks by moving their bodies as if they were popping, jumping, springing and sparkling!

Explain to the children that they have to start and stop when they see you make a special signal, for example, when you raise your hands in the air or when you raise a picture of a firework and wave it. Let the children swap roles and repeat the activity, perhaps changing the special signal.

Extend the activity by inviting the children to move around the room to represent a spinning Catherine wheel or a rocket flying through the air.

Encourage the children to put a sequence of three different movements together, for example, a 'pop', 'run' and 'spin' or a 'twirl', 'spring' and 'sparkle'. Talk about the children's physical interpretation of the words.

Support
Let the children have some free time using the instruments beforehand so that they can find out how to handle and use the instruments safely and correctly.

Extension
Arrange the children so that they gradually build up sound. For example, the first child could play their instrument followed by the second child, followed by the third and so on.

Alternatively, show the children hand signals as a very basic introduction to watching a conductor to determine quiet sounds such as holding your hands down low, or loud sounds by holding your hands up high.

Tartan teddies

What you need
The photocopiable sheet on page 76; a selection of tartan fabric; a variety of tartan garments; dress pins or double-sided sticky tape; scissors; fabric glue or needle and thread; small pieces of felt; soft-toy stuffing.

Preparation
Make an A3 or A4 copy of the photocopiable sheet for each child.

What to do
Talk with the children about the traditions and celebrations enjoyed by Scottish people on St Andrew's Day. Show the group the different examples of tartan fabric and tartan garments. Explain that tartan is a special fabric that is traditional to Scotland.

Give each child an A3 or A4 copy of the photocopiable sheet and help them to cut around the thick black line to create a paper teddy template, and to pin it on a piece of tartan fabric. Alternatively, use doubled-sided sticky tape to secure the template to the tartan.

Help each child to cut out two fabric teddy shapes and glue or sew around the edge leaving a small gap for stuffing. Ask them to carefully place a small amount of soft-toy stuffing into the gap. Help them to sew or glue the gap together and to cut out and glue felt features such as eyes, nose and mouth onto their teddies.

Encourage the children to use their 'Tartan teddies' for imaginative play such as a tartan teddy bears' picnic.

Invite them to 'sit' their teddies on a tartan rug. Provide, or let the children make, tartan-style napkins or paper plates. Use real or pretend food.

Follow-up the activity by introducing the children to traditions generally associated with Scottish people, for example, listening to Scottish music or making St Andrew's flags (blue background with a white cross).

Show the children where Scotland is on a map of Britain and then point to Britain on a globe. Explain to the children where other countries are according to their own interests, for example, a holiday destination, where Grandma lives and so on.

Support
Provide the children with hand-over-hand support during the soft-toy stuffing stages.

Extension
Encourage the children to use their 'Tartan teddies' to help them act out a narrative during role-play.

If you have enough tartan fabric, invite the children to use it to make accessories for their teddies, such as a bow ties, jackets or hats.

Learning objectives
To use ideas involving fitting, overlapping, in and out; to play alongside other children who are engaged in the same theme.

Group size
Individuals or small groups.

Home links
Let the children take their 'Tartan teddies' home. Ask parents and carers if they have any tartan garments or items for a 'Scottish theme' display.

Hanukkah candlestick

Learning objectives
To make a three-dimensional structure; to work creatively on a small scale.

Group size
Nine children

What you need
Air-drying clay; clay boards; small cardboard discs approximately 5cm in diameter; poster paint; paintbrushes; glitter glue, or PVA glue and glitter mixed together; glue brush; red and yellow tissue paper; stripy plastic straws cut into lengths of approximately 5cm; child scissors; aprons; small pot of water or damp sponge; low table.

What to do
Talk to the children about the Jewish festival of Hanukkah. Explain to them that they are going to make Hanukkah candlesticks to celebrate this Festival of Light.

Give each child a small lump of clay and a cardboard disc and ask them to roll the clay into a ball, then to sit it in the centre of their disc. Invite them to press a length of plastic straw into their clay to represent a candle and leave in a safe place to dry.

When the clay is completely dry, provide poster paints and glitter glue and invite the children to use their creative imagination to decorate their models with colourful shapes, lines, dots and patterns. Encourage each child to add a flame to their candlestick by gluing small twists of red and yellow

tissue paper into the top of the straw. Invite the children to place eight of the candles in a row along a low table and explain that each candle represents one day of the festival of Hanukkah. Then, place the ninth candle in the middle of the row and say that this candle is called the 'servant candle' and is used to light the other candles during the eight-day celebration. Use the display to inspire role-play based on the festival of Hanukkah.

Alternatively, encourage the children to use the display for an observational painting, showing all nine candles.

Support
Make sure that the clay is soft for the children to manipulate. Hold the model still during the modelling stage to prevent the children from getting frustrated in case it begins to wobble or fall over.

Extension
Invite the children to create textured patterns in the clay using clay tools or create designs using paint effects such as curls, wavy lines and pictures.

Keeping warm

What you need
The photocopiable sheet on page 77; piano or guitar for an adult to play (optional); a tape of someone singing 'The keeping warm song' (optional).

What to do
Sing 'The keeping warm song' on the photocopiable sheet to the children. If possible, accompany your singing with a musical instrument such as a piano or guitar. Alternatively, play a tape recording of the song to the children.

Talk with the children about the words in the song. Explain to them that the first four verses are about getting dressed for outdoor play, and the second four verses are about how to keep warm while outside.

Ask the children if the song is about cold days or warm days, winter or summer. Talk to them about the type of actions that they could perform to accompany each verse.

For example:

Verse 1:   Mime putting on a hat.
Verse 2:   Mime putting on a coat.
Verse 3:   Mime putting on gloves.
Verse 4:   Mime putting on a scarf.
Verse 5:   Stamp feet.
Verse 6:   Jump up and down.
Verse 7:   Wave arms around.
Verse 8:   Run on the spot.

Sing the song with the children and carry out the actions.

Alternatively, provide a selection of hats, gloves, coats and scarves for the children to put on as they listen to a tape recording of the song.

Follow up the activity by inviting the children to play instruments while they sing the song. Make a tape of the children singing and playing their instruments. Alternatively, help the children to make their own musical instruments to accompany the song.

Support
Encourage the children to copy your movements as the whole group joins in the song.

Extension
Invite the children to draw a picture plan to remind them of the actions and the order of the verses. For example, the first picture could show a woolly hat, the second picture gloves, and so on.

Learning objective
To imitate and create movement in response to a song.

Group size
Small or large group.

Home links
Make a copy of the song for the children to take home and sing at home with their families. Invite parents and carers in to watch the children perform the actions and words to 'The keeping warm song'.

Winter scenes

Learning objective
To try to capture experiences and responses with paint and other materials.

Group size
Small groups.

What you need
Winter and snowy scene pictures; paints; painting materials; felt-tipped pens or coloured pencils; flip chart or large sheet of paper; display board at the children's height; black and white A3 painting paper; black and white mounting paper slightly larger than A3; glue; silver paper or foil; blue and grey backing paper; scissors; aprons.

Preparation
Cover a display board in bold alternate stripes of blue and grey backing paper.

What to do
Show the children the winter and snowy scene pictures. Talk about the colours in the pictures. Which colours do the children associate with cold weather? Use felt-tipped pens or coloured pencils to make a picture list of 'cold colours' on a flip chart, for example, a patch of grey, white, blue, dark grey and so on.

Provide paints and painting equipment and encourage the children to mix different colours together to make some 'cold colours'. Give each child a piece of black or white painting paper and invite them to paint a picture or a pattern using their prepared 'cold colours'.

When the paintings are dry, help the children to mount them onto paper of an opposite colour, for example, a painting on black paper can be mounted onto white paper and vice versa. Display the paintings on a display board at the children's height. Encourage the children to cut strips of silver paper or foil to hang across the display to represent icicles.

Use the display to inspire discussion about winter weather. Can the children recall playing in the snow, walking in the rain, or finding icicles on windows?'.

Follow up the activity by inviting each child to paint a picture showing an indoor scene during winter. Talk about the colours that they could use to represent a warm kitchen, a cosy living room or a snuggly bedroom. Display each picture with drapes of fabric on either side to represent curtains. Explain to the children that the pictures depict a view through a window on a cold winter's day or night.

Support
Help the children during the colour-mixing stage. Talk about light and dark shades and encourage the children to identify the different colours as they are mixed.

Extension
Invite the children to make paper snowflakes to hang in front of the display.

Weather chart

What you need
The photocopiable sheet on page 78; felt-tipped pens or coloured pencils; white card approximately 15cm x 11cm; large sheet of paper or whiteboard labelled with the words 'Today it is…'; Blu-Tack; storage box or basket, large enough to hold the white cards.

Preparation
Make an enlarged copy of the weather chart on the photocopiable sheet and display this during the week before carrying out the activity. Help the children to keep a record of the week's weather by asking them to take turns to draw a circle around the appropriate weather symbol(s) each day.

What to do
During a cold winter's day, gather the children together and talk about the weather. Ask, 'What is the weather like today?', 'What has the weather been like this week?', 'What other types of winter weather can you recall?'.

Refer to the weather chart that the children completed during the previous week as a visual aid and to jog their memories about different types of winter weather.

Give the children some pieces of white card and ask them to draw their own weather symbols. Then look together at all the different symbols that the children have drawn. Encourage them to guess what each other's symbols represent.

Store the symbols in a box and use them to record the weather each morning by inviting the children to attach the appropriate symbols on a large sheet of paper or whiteboard with Blu-Tack, labelled with the words 'Today it is…'.

Support
Let the children to copy the symbols from the enlarged photocopiable sheet.

Extension
Invite the children to think of original weather symbols, suggesting ideas that are different from those on the photocopiable sheet – perhaps a raincoat for a rainy day.

Learning objective
To begin to use representation as a means of communication.

Group size
Whole group.

Home links
Encourage parents and carers to help their children develop their observational skills by asking them to look out for signs and symbols while they are out and about. For example, pictorial road signs, road signs with numbers, signs and symbols on shop doors and windows, signs in buses, at railway stations and so on.

Santa's grotto

What you need
Role-play area; resources for Santa's grotto such as strips of crêpe paper, plastic or fabric playhouse, chair, fabric drapes and Christmas decorations; a child-sized Santa outfit or dressing-up clothes such as a red jacket with hood, fake beard, black boots, small cushion for tummy padding and large belt; elf and reindeer outfits or dressing-up

clothes such as a green jacket, green hat, green trousers and belt for an elf, a brown jumper, brown trousers, brown gloves, brown socks or shoes, a brown plastic hairband with 'antlers' cut from card attached to the rim with sticky tape for a reindeer; sack; empty boxes; sticky tape; wrapping paper; dolls.

Preparation
Position the plastic or fabric playhouse and chair in the role-play area and

invite the children to wrap empty boxes to create pretend presents to put into Santa's sack.

What to do
Talk with the children about their favourite preparations and special times during the run-up to Christmas, for example, visiting Santa's grotto. Invite them to create Santa's grotto in the role-play area.

Provide a wide selection of available resources and materials. For example, a simple but effective grotto can be achieved by covering the outside of a playhouse in colourful fabric drapes, then hanging several strips of crêpe paper down the roof and walls. Invite the children to tape Christmas decorations to the strips of crêpe paper. Next, cover a child's chair in red fabric and place a sack full of 'presents' near to the chair.

When the grotto is complete, invite the children to take it in turns to dress up as Santa, an elf and reindeer.

Provide the rest of the children with dolls to represent young children. Invite the group to act as the parents or carers taking their children to see Santa in the grotto to receive 'presents' from Santa's sack.

Support
Help the children to decorate the role-play area.

Extension
Invite the children to introduce a story-line or narrative into their role-play.

On a cold and frosty morning

What you need
Five instruments such as a shaker, triangle, tambourine, bells and drum; a comfortable place to sit; a piece of card approximately 30cm x 30cm; dowelling rod approximately 30cm; coloured pens; the song and tune of 'Here We Go Round the Mulberry Bush' from *This Little Puffin…* compiled by Elizabeth Matterson (Puffin Books).

Preparation
Make a giant spinner from a piece of card showing six pictures on both sides, for example, five different instruments and a pair of hands clapping. Make a hole in the middle of the spinner and insert the dowelling rod.

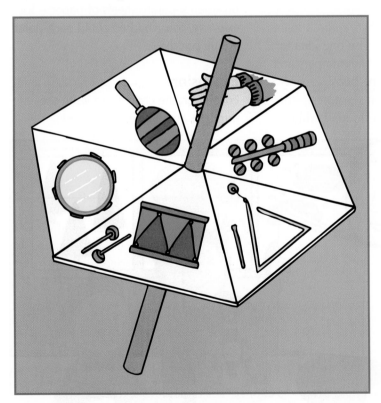

appearance of the winter's morning. Introduce terms such as frosty, chilly and freezing.

Invite the children to join in singing two verses of 'Here We Go Round the Mulberry Bush'. Share the instruments among the children and explain that those without an instrument can clap their hands.

Place the giant spinner on the floor in the middle of the circle and invite a child to spin it. If the spinner lands on a picture of a shaker, for example, all the children holding a shaker should play their instruments while the others sing 'This is the way we play our shakers, play our shakers, play our shakers, this is the way we play our shakers on a cold and frosty morning'. If the spinner lands on the picture of the pair of hands clapping, invite all the children to clap their hands while they sing 'This is the way we clap our hands…'. Repeat the activity several times and swap the instruments around between verses to make sure that everyone has a turn at playing an instrument.

What to do
During a cold, winter morning, gather the children together in a large circle. Talk about the wintry weather outside. Ask, 'Who walked to the setting today?' or 'Was it icy, wet, windy?'. Encourage the children to describe the feel and

Support
Show the children how to handle and play each instrument correctly.

Extension
Involve the children in helping to make the spinner.

Learning objective
To explore the different sounds of instruments.

Group size
Large or small groups.

Home links
Ask parents and carers who can play an instrument to show and play their instruments for the children.

Invite parents and carers to a mini music concert where the children can play instruments and sing songs that they have learned.

Ten white snowflakes

What you need
A sheet of A1 coloured card; three sheets of A1 white paper; stapler; A3 paper; glue; paints; painting materials; scissors; thick marker pen; flip chart or whiteboard.

Preparation
Fold three pieces of A1 white paper inside a piece of A1 coloured card to make a big book, and secure them with a stapler.

What to do
Ask the children to think of ten things that can be seen in winter. Write their ideas on a flip chart or whiteboard. Explain that you are going to make a winter counting book.

Decide with the children on a main colour for each idea. Use one idea for each page and write the numbers and words straight into the book, leaving space for the children's pictures – for example, 1 grey rain cloud, 2 white snowmen, 3 green fir trees, 4 blue puddles, 5 black footprints, 6 blue raindrops and so on.

Provide the children with A3 paper and coloured paints and invite them to paint some pictures to illustrate the book. Help them to recall how many things they need to include in their picture. When the paintings are dry, help the children to match the correct pictures to the wording in the big book. Spare pictures can be cut out and used to decorate the front and back covers of the book. Use it as an ongoing resource to reinforce counting skills.

Support
Invite the children to paint each picture on small separate sheets of paper – for example, four children could each paint a blue puddle.

Extension
Encourage the children to write the numbers and words in the book.

Giant Advent calendar

What you need
Display board; black backing paper; hole-punch; 25 sheets of thick white paper or card approximately 20cm x 20cm each; 12 sheets of green paper and 13 sheets of red paper approximately 20cm x 20cm each; 13 pieces of green ribbon wool and 12 pieces of red ribbon approximately 25cm in length; red and green poster paints; coloured pens; pencil crayons; pastel crayons; glitter; glue; Christmas-themed pictures from old Christmas cards; an Advent calendar.

Preparation
Cover a display board in black backing paper. Use a hole-punch to make two holes in the centre top of each square of paper.

What to do
Explain to the children what Advent is. Show them an Advent calendar and tell them that from the first day of December a 'door' is opened every day until Christmas Day.

Tell the children that they are going to make a giant Advent calendar. Share the 25 sheets of white paper or card among the children and ask them to draw a winter or Christmas scene on each piece of paper using coloured pens, pencils or pastels. Provide a selection of old Christmas cards to inspire ideas.

Next, help the children to decorate each picture using glue and glitter. Invite them to thread lengths of green ribbon through the holes in 13 pictures, and lengths of red ribbon through 12 pictures. Arrange all the pictures onto the black backing paper in a 13cm x 13cm grid.

Ask the children to use green paint to label the red squares of paper with odd numbers 1 to 25 and red paint to label the green squares of paper with

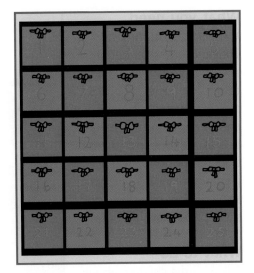

even numbers 2 to 24. When the paint is dry, tie the coloured labels in numerical order onto each picture to create a 'door'.

During December, Invite the children to open one 'door' each day on the giant Advent calendar to reveal a picture.

Support
Let the children cut and stick pictures from old Christmas cards onto the white paper or card.

Extension
Invite the children to help assemble the display by threading the labels and tying the ribbons.

Learning objective
To use ideas involving fitting, overlapping, in, out, enclosure and grids.

Group size
Up to 25 children.

Home links
Help the children to make 'lift-the-flap' Christmas cards. Ask parents and carers to encourage their children to write in their cards at home and then to help them address and stamp an envelope for their card and post it to a friend or relative.

Tree decorations

What you need

A small, real or artificial Christmas tree; salt dough; winter or Christmas-shapes cutters such as stars, circles, crescents, trees, snowmen and so on; protective mats or boards; rolling-pins; bright-coloured poster paints; painting materials; varnish; shiny ribbon; glue; gold and silver paper stars; aprons.

What to do

Talk with the children about the festivities associated with Christmas Day. Explain that part of the tradition of Christmas is to decorate a Christmas tree.

Show the children a small 'bare' Christmas tree and invite them to make some colourful decorations to hang on its branches. Give each child a fist-sized piece of salt dough and a rolling-pin and ask them to roll it flat, then to choose some cutters to make salt-dough shapes. Encourage the children to talk about the feel of the dough as they manipulate it with their fingers. Help each child to poke a small hole in the top of each dough shape, and leave to dry.

Provide a wide selection of bright-coloured poster paints. Encourage the children to use their creative imagination to decorate their salt-dough shapes, for example, with spots, stripes, dots, zigzag patterns or random patterns. Let the paint dry before decorating the other side. When both sides are painted and dry, invite the children to glue a few small, shiny stars onto their shapes.

Finally, assist each child with the varnishing of their shape and the threading of a shiny ribbon through the

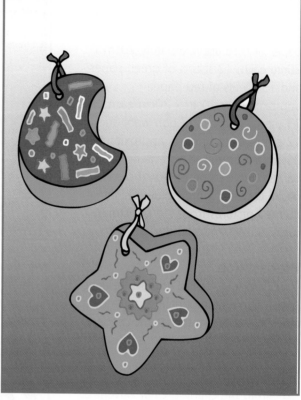

hole in the top to create a hanging decoration for the Christmas tree.

Ask the children to sit in a circle around the tree and encourage them to look at the variety of hand-made decorations and to compare the different shapes, colours and designs. Ask questions such as, 'Can you see a star shape?', 'How many circles can you see?', 'Are there more red decorations than blue?', 'How many different types of shapes are there?', 'Can you name the shapes?' and so on.

Support

Invite the children to paint their shapes with just one colour before adding the shiny stars.

Extension

Invite the children to use fine paintbrushes to decorate their shapes with a simple Christmas picture such as a holly leaf or a snowflake.

Learning objectives
To show an interest in what they see, touch and feel; to make comparisons.

Group size
Small groups.

Shiny crescents

What you need
The photocopiable sheet on page 80; a range of gold and silver collage materials such as ribbon, paper, braid, shiny sticky tape, foil, sequins, glitter; gold and silver pens, pencils and crayons; glue; scissors; A3 black card (folded in half); A4 or A5 white paper, black, silver or gold pen or pencil.

Preparation
Make a copy of the photocopiable sheet for each child.

What to do
Talk to the children about the festival of Eid-ul-Fitr which is celebrated by Muslims at the end of the month of Ramadan. Explain that as part of the celebrations, family and friends send cards to one another.

Invite the children to make an Eid card. Give each child a copy of the photocopiable sheet, an assortment of collage materials and gold and silver pens and pencils. Encourage each child to decorate the crescent shape by covering all the available space in gold and silver.

Give suggestions for decorating the crescent shape such as colouring the whole crescent using pens or crayons then overlaying with sequins or shiny paper; dividing the crescent shape into sections then decorating each section using a different medium or filling the crescent with small shapes cut from shiny paper to create a tessellating or mosaic pattern.

When the crescents are complete, give each child a sheet of A3 black card folded in half. Explain that Arabic and Urdu are read from left to right and that the card needs to open on the left-hand side. Help each child to cut out and glue their decorated crescent onto the front of the card. Provide them with an A4 or A5 sheet of white paper and a black, silver or gold pen or pencil. Help them to write a short 'To' and 'From' message on the paper to glue inside the card.

Support
If the children find it difficult to cut out the crescent shape, help them to just trim off the top of the photocopiable sheet where the heading is.

Extension
Make a crescent-shaped template for the children to draw around.

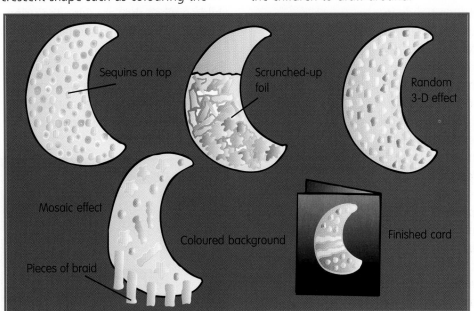

Sequins on top

Scrunched-up foil

Random 3-D effect

Mosaic effect

Coloured background

Pieces of braid

Finished card

Calendar keepsake

What you need
A piece of A5 plain, cotton fabric for each child; cold-water dye; string or elastic bands; bucket; rubber gloves; iron (for adult use); A5 card; A5 card frame; glue; small calendars; hole-punch; ribbon in a colour to match the dye; large button, bead or plastic brick; sticky tape.

Preparation
Prepare the cold-water dye as described on the packet and ensure that you store it in a safe place.

What to do
Talk with the children about the meaning of New Year. Show them a calendar and explain that 1 January is the first day of the New Year. Invite them to make a 'calendar keepsake'. Give each child a small piece of fabric and ask them to lay a large button, bead or small plastic brick in the centre of the fabric. Next, invite them to use a piece of string or an elastic band to tie the

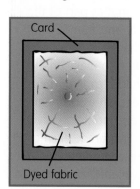

button tightly in the middle of the fabric. Then, ask them to tie two or more lengths of string or elastic bands around the excess fabric until it resembles a 'sausage shape'.

String or elastic band

Place each piece of tied fabric into the dye according to the instructions on the packet. Invite the children to watch as the tied fabric is removed from the dye. Leave it in a safe, warm place to dry.

Help each child to untie the string or elastic bands. Encourage them to look at the 'sun-like' patterns that radiate across the fabric and to observe the variety of designs. Iron each piece of fabric away from the children.

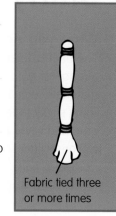

Fabric tied three or more times

Next, ask each child to glue the edges of an A5 sheet of card and help them to smooth their tie-and-dye design over the card.

Finally, give each child an A5 card frame and invite them to carefully glue their design to the frame and leave it to dry. Encourage them to tape a small calendar along the bottom edge of the frame and a loop of ribbon at the top for hanging.

Card

Dyed fabric

Support
Provide plenty of assistance to the children when they are tying the string or elastic band around the fabric.

Extension
Invite the children to help with the preparation stages such as cutting the fabric, collecting the buttons or beads, stirring the dye and so on.

calendar

Field of yellow

Learning objective
To understand that different media can be combined.

Group size
Large or small groups.

What you need
Sheets of A3 or A4 pale yellow paper; a range of colouring materials in dark and light shades of yellow; an assortment of collage materials cut into strips, for example, paper, plain fabric, patterned fabric, ribbon, card, tissue paper, crêpe paper and so on; glue; pictures of spring showing fields of yellow flowers; display board.

What to do
Talk with the children about the Hindu festival of Saraswati Puja, which celebrates the start of spring when the fields in India are full of yellow flowers. Explain to them that, from a distance, these fields resemble a huge canvas covered in shades of yellow. Invite the children to create a large display in shades of yellow to represent these fields in India.

Give each child an A3 or A4 sheet of pale yellow paper and a wide selection of materials in light and dark shades of yellow. Allow them a high degree of independence as they experiment with

creating an abstract design using the mixed media. Encourage them to colour their paper using an assortment of drawing materials in various shades of yellow, and to stick, dangle and entwine a variety of collage strips across the paper to create a 3-D effect. Other suggestions for manipulating the collage strips could include overlapping, twisting, scrunching, looping and waving.

When the designs are complete, use them to cover a display board, making sure that there are no gaps, to represent a field of yellow flowers that you can see in India. Encourage the children to talk about the display and view it from a distance.

Support
Show the children how to loop, twist, weave, overlap and scrunch the different materials.

Extension
Invite the children to help you assemble the display.

Home links
Encourage parents and carers to visit a library with their children to look at books about India or abstract art.

Hanging banners

What you need
Sheets of red, white and yellow A3 paper; bright red, black, yellow or gold paints; painting materials; black A3 mounting paper; gold paper, foil or wrapping paper; small rectangles of stiff card approximately 4cm x 6cm; sharp scissors (adult use only); child-safe scissors; glue; red, yellow or gold thread; books about Chinese New Year; examples of Chinese writing; pencil; long ruler; red or gold glitter; protective table covering; aprons.

Preparation
Cut the sheets of red, white and yellow A3 paper in half vertically to create strips, and cut slightly larger strips from the black mounting paper. Then create 'card combs' by cutting strips

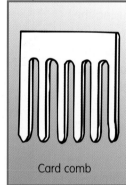
Card comb

along the rectangles of stiff card. Snip the ends along the 'comb' to create a jagged 'tooth' effect. Finally, draw a border that is approximately 5cm wide around the edge of each paper strip using a ruler and pencil.

What to do
Talk with the children about the customs associated with the festival of Chinese New Year. Look at the books about Chinese New Year together and show the children some examples of traditional Chinese writing.

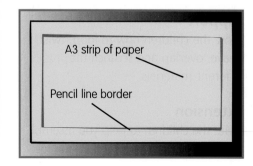
A3 strip of paper

Pencil line border

Invite the children to make a Chinese-style banner. Cover a table with a protective covering. Give each child an A3 strip of red, yellow or white paper, a 'card comb' and trays of paint in red, yellow or gold. Invite them to dip the 'card comb' into the paint and to drag it around the edge of their paper to create a decorative border. Leave to dry.

Invite each child to paint some Chinese-style writing down the centre of their paper using the black paint. When the paint is dry, encourage the children to add red or gold glitter around the border. Leave to dry once more, then mount the pictures back to back on strips of black mounting paper.

Show each child how to 'fringe' a strip of gold paper, foil or wrapping paper to glue along the bottom edge of their picture. Add red or gold thread to the top of the pictures and hang them in the room to create a banner to honour Chinese New Year.

Support
Help the children during the 'combing' stage by guiding their hands gently along their papers.

Extension
Invite the children to design a 'banner'. Encourage them to think about an interesting 'border' design, or to consider using Chinese-style pictures instead of 'writing' down the centre of their banner.

Black mounting paper

Child's picture

Gold 'fringe' effect

Mobile hearts

What you need
Sheets of red, white, light-pink and dark-pink A4 card; red, pink, white, lilac, purple, maroon pencils or pens; glue; thread or string; streamers such as narrow strips of florist ribbon; tissue or crêpe paper in similar shades to the pen colours; tiny paper or fabric heart shapes approximately 3cm x 3cm.

Preparation
Cut out four hearts approximately 20cm x 20cm from the sheets of red, white, light pink and dark pink card for each child.

What to do
Talk with the children about the traditions of Valentine's Day and invite them to create a display of 'Valentine mobiles'.

Give each child four card heart shapes and invite them to use coloured pens and pencils to decorate one side of each heart shape. Then show the children how to fold all four hearts in half, making sure that the decorated section is on the inside of the fold.

Next, help each child to glue the reverse side of all four folded hearts together to create one three-dimensional decorated heart shape.

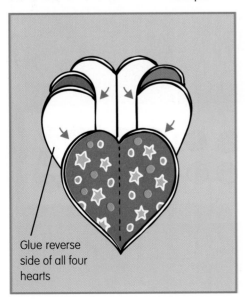

Glue reverse side of all four hearts

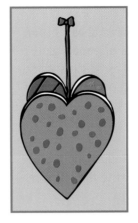

Attach string or coloured thread to the top of the heart to create a mobile that will twist and twirl in the breeze.

Invite the children to help create a mobile display by tying several 3-D hearts to one or more lengths of string secured across the room.

Encourage the children to help you cut out tiny paper heart shapes and glue them to both ends of several fine 'streamers' to decorate in between each 3-D heart, draping the streamers over the string.

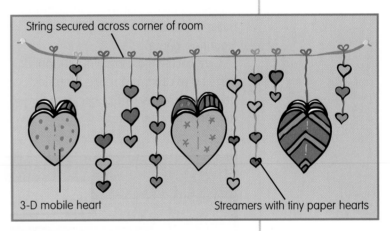

String secured across corner of room

3-D mobile heart   Streamers with tiny paper hearts

Support
Provide the children with hand-over-hand assistance during the folding and gluing stages. Invite them to make random marks or patterns on each heart shape.

Extension
Ask the children to cut out their own paper and card heart shapes using heart-shaped templates. Encourage them to think of a different picture or pattern that they could draw on each of the four hearts.

Learning objective
To make three-dimensional structures.

Group size
Small groups.

Home links
Encourage parents and carers to provide their children with an assortment of colourful paper or card so that they can explore making 2-D and 3-D constructions at home.

Pancake counting line

What you need
Three different-coloured sheets of A4 card; 21 yellow discs of paper; glue; brown felt-tipped pens; scissors; thick marker pen; backing paper; examples of real pancakes.

Preparation
Cut each sheet of A4 card into four equal sections and write the numbers 1 to 6 on six of the cards.

What to do
Talk to the children about Shrove Tuesday and tell them that it is also known as Pancake Day. Ask them to wash their hands, and let them taste the pancakes that you have already prepared. Encourage them to tell you how the pancakes look and taste, and explain to them that they are going to make a 'pancake counting line' and 'counting game'.

Give each child a brown felt-tipped pen and ask them to make 'speckles' on the yellow discs of paper until they resemble tiny pancakes.

Help each child to glue a 'pancake' onto one of the blank cards which colour matches card number '1', then two 'pancakes' on card number 2, and so on, up to six 'pancakes' on the sixth card. Leave to dry, then ask the children to sort and match the 'number cards' to the correct 'pancake cards'.

Invite the children to place the cards in the correct order along a strip of backing paper to create a 'number line'. Display it at the children's height and use it as an ongoing shared resource during number activities.

Alternatively, use the cards as large playing cards to play a matching game such as 'Pairs'.

Support
Help the children to make giant-sized cards using large 'fabric pancakes' and 12 A4 sheets of card.

Extension
Invite the children to make a set of coloured cards showing numbers up to 10 or more.

Learning objective
To work and play alongside other children who are engaged in the same theme.

Group size
Up to six children.

Home links
Ask parents and carers to let their children help to make pancake mixture at home.

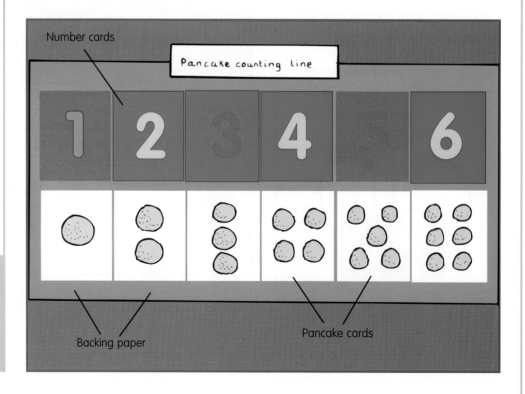

Number cards

Pancake counting line

Backing paper

Pancake cards

Spring is here!

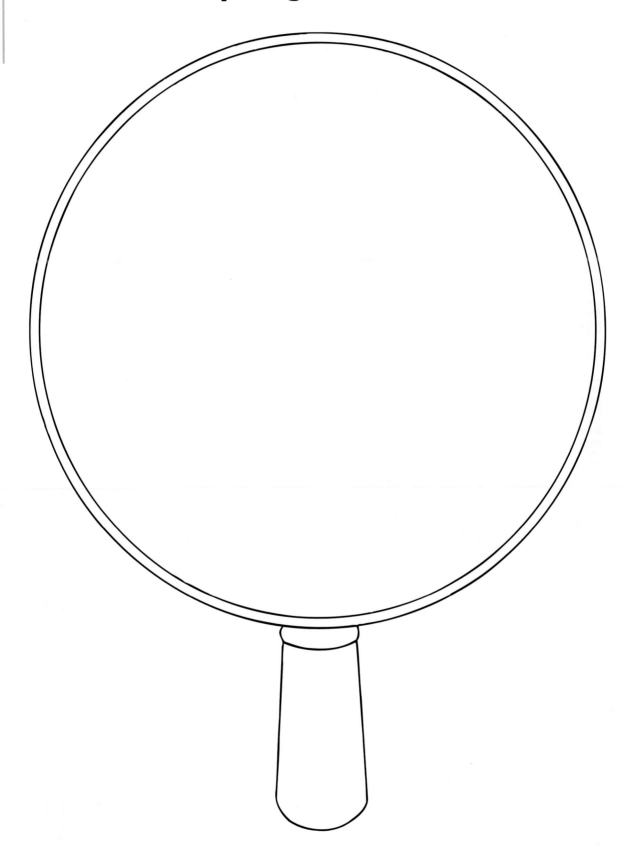

Happy hands

Once there were so many
of my handprints we could see,
on windows, doors and other things
left by busy, sticky me!

But one day soon, this will change
as I am growing fast,
no more smudges, smears and fingerprints
those sticky days will pass!

So here's a little keepsake
of my handprints from today,
to look at in the future,
when there're none to wipe away!

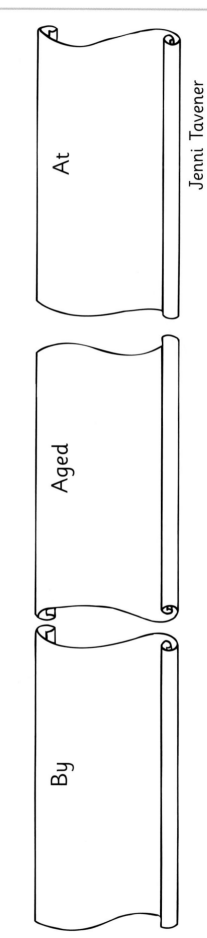

At

Aged

By

Jenni Tavener

Veggie colours

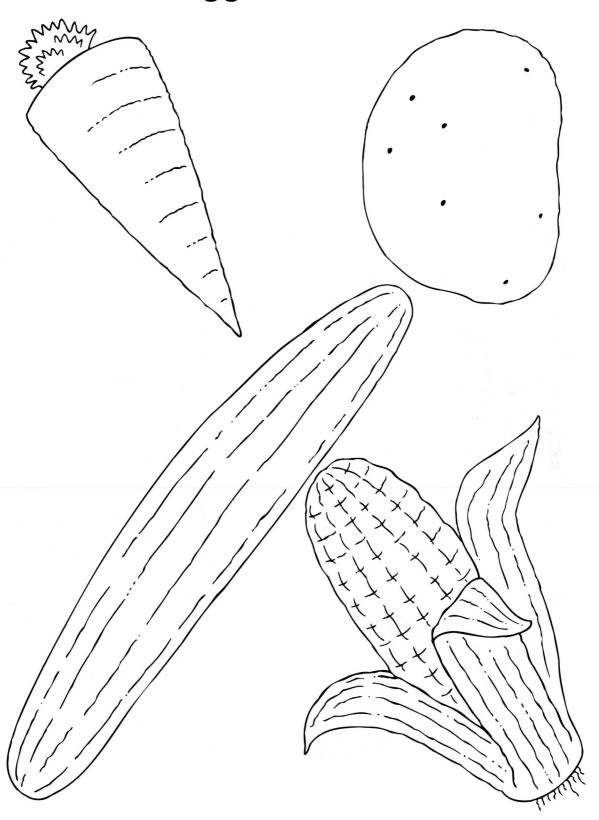

Floral patterns

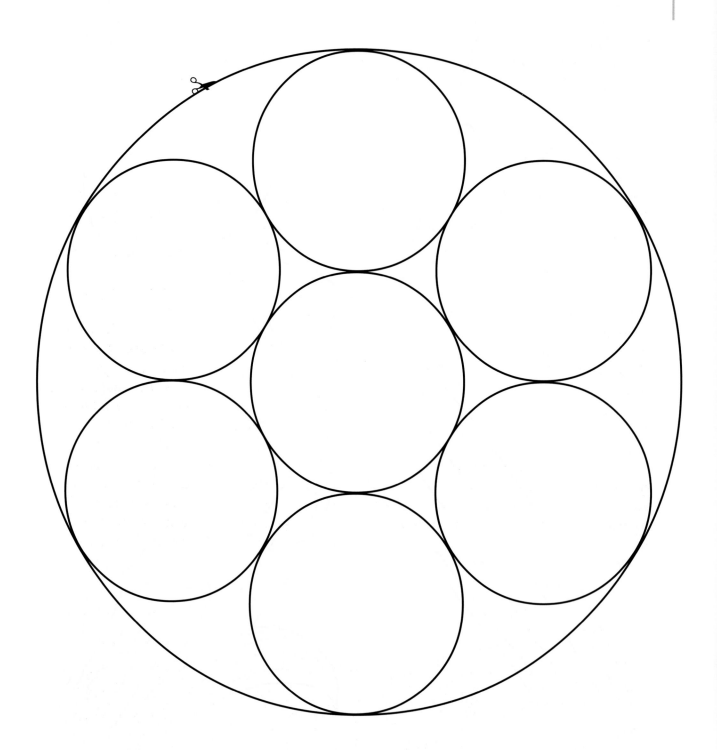

Mr Goodman's garden

From Monday to Friday, Mr Goodman worked all day long in a stuffy office, so in the evenings and during the weekend, he liked to spend all his spare time in the garden. Mr Goodman had a very long garden. At one end of the garden was his house, and at the other end was a beautiful river. Right in the middle of the garden was a very, very big, old tree. This was Mr Goodman's favourite tree.

One day, Mr Goodman decided that he would like some flowers in his garden. So, he planted many flower bulbs and sowed a lot of seeds. Mr Goodman worked very hard to look after his seeds and bulbs, and he watered them regularly.

When summer arrived, the flowers had not grown. Mr Goodman was very disappointed, so he tried again. Although he worked hard to look after his bulbs and seeds, once again no flowers grew.

One autumn night there was a terrible storm. Mr Goodman could hear the wind howling and the trees creaking. Then, he heard a terrible crash. Mr Goodman rushed outside to see what had happened. His favourite, big old tree had blown down. Mr Goodman was very sad.

During the following spring, Mr Goodman noticed something strange happening in his garden. He noticed small shoots, and soon some flowers began to grow. By the time summer had arrived, Mr Goodman's garden was full of beautiful flowers. The flowers stretched all the way down the garden between the house and the river. Mr Goodman was very puzzled! But then he realized that the big old tree that used to sit in the middle of the lawn had kept the garden in shade and the flowers could not grow without sunlight. So, although Mr Goodman had lost his favourite tree, he had gained a garden full of colourful flowers.

Jenni Tavener

T-shirt patch

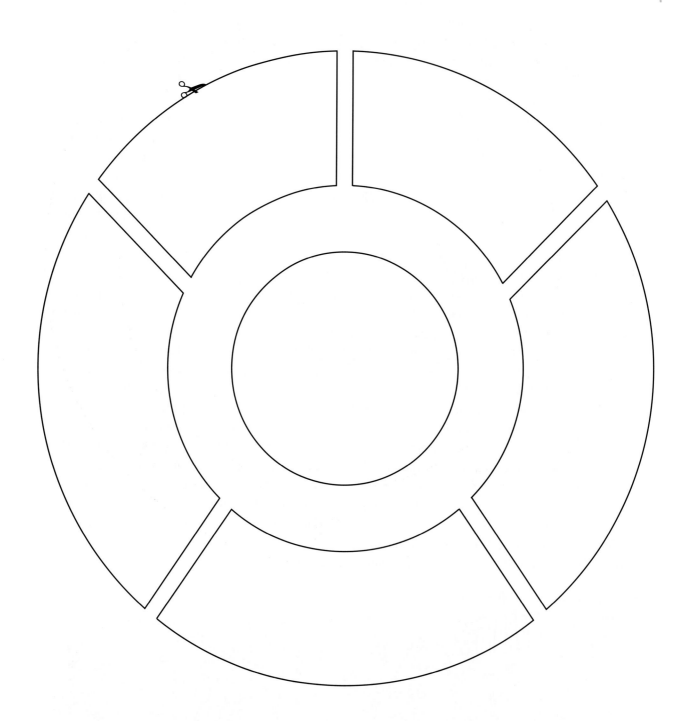

Someone special

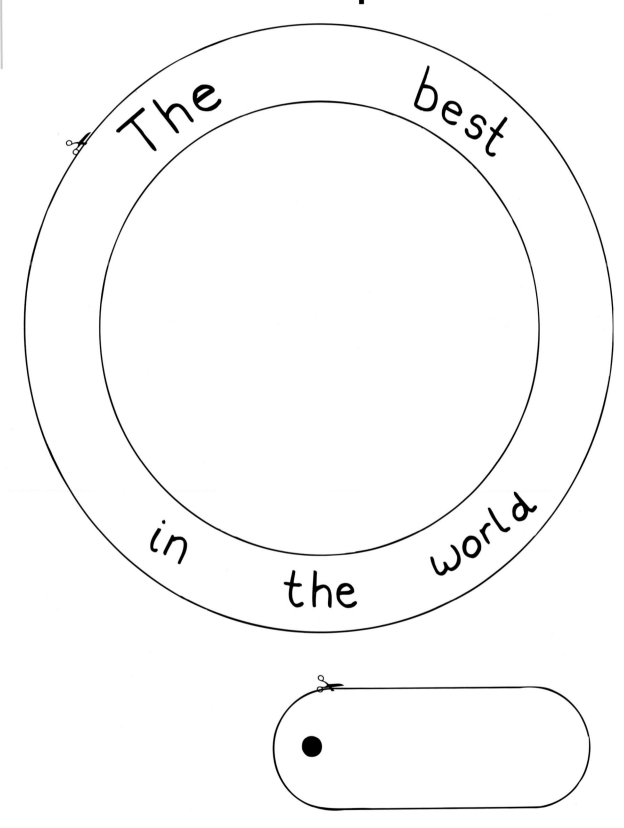

Midnight stars

Autumn changes

Coloured leaves, shake and fall,
Hedgehogs curl into a ball.

Morning mists and round red sun,
Bonfires, chestnuts, having fun!

Squirrels scamper here and there,
Nuts and acorns everywhere.

Other days, it's wind and rain,
Splashy puddles in the lane.

Pretty fir cones close up tight,
Children have a conker fight!

Summer birds flock together,
Soon to leave our colder weather.

Autumn changes in the air,
Autumn days for us to share.

Brenda Williams

Autumn colours

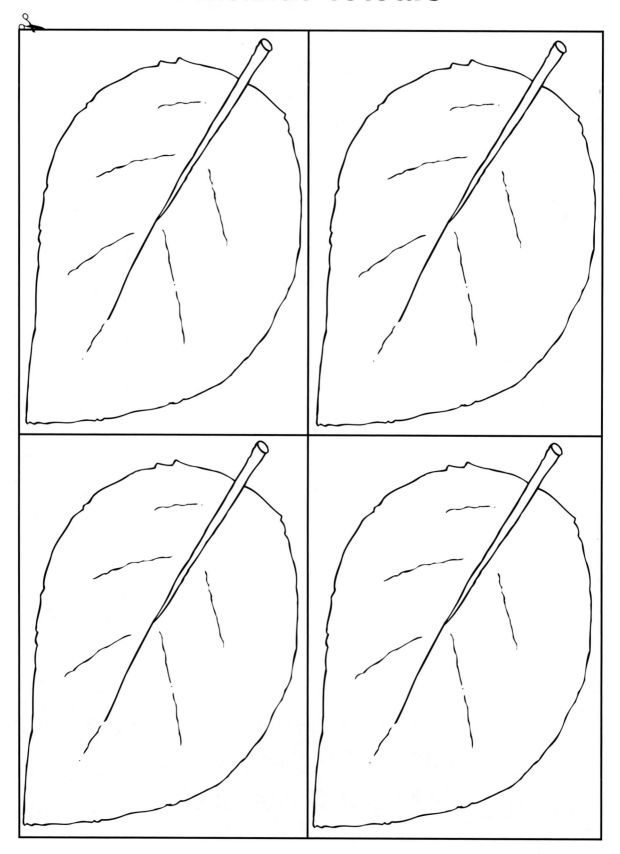

A photo for you

Here's my little fingers
Here's my little thumbs

Here's a little picture
of your 'little one'!

Tartan teddies

The keeping warm song

(Tune: 'Here We Go Round the Mulberry Bush')

F   **C7**

1. Now I put on my wool - ly hat, Wool - ly hat, wool - ly hat.

F   **C7**   **F**

Now I put on my wool - ly hat, To keep__ me warm.

2. Now I put on my coat,
Put on my coat, put on my coat,
Now I put on my coat,
To keep me warm.

3. Now I tuck my hands in my gloves,
Hands in gloves, hands in gloves,
Now I tuck my hands in my gloves,
To keep me warm.

4. Now I wrap up in a scarf,
Wrap up in a scarf, wrap up in a scarf,
Now I wrap up in a scarf,
To keep me warm.

5. Now I quickly stamp my feet,
Stamp my feet, stamp my feet,
Now I quickly stamp my feet,
To keep me warm.

6. Now I'm jumping up and down,
Up and down, up and down,
Now I'm jumping up and down,
To keep me warm.

7. Now I'm waving my arms around,
Arms around, arms around,
Now I'm waving my arms around,
To keep me warm.

8. Now I'm running about,
Running about, running about,
Now I'm running about,
To keep me warm.

Jenni Tavener

Weather chart

Draw a circle around the symbols which match today's weather.

Monday	rainy	sunny	snowy	windy	cloudy
Tuesday	rainy	sunny	snowy	windy	cloudy
Wednesday	rainy	sunny	snowy	windy	cloudy
Thursday	rainy	sunny	snowy	windy	cloudy
Friday	rainy	sunny	snowy	windy	cloudy

Key:  rainy    sunny   snowy   windy   cloudy

Gift tags

Colour and cut out the gift tags to attach to Christmas presents for family or friends.

To _____

From _____

To _____

From _____

To _____

From _____

To _____

From _____

Shiny crescents

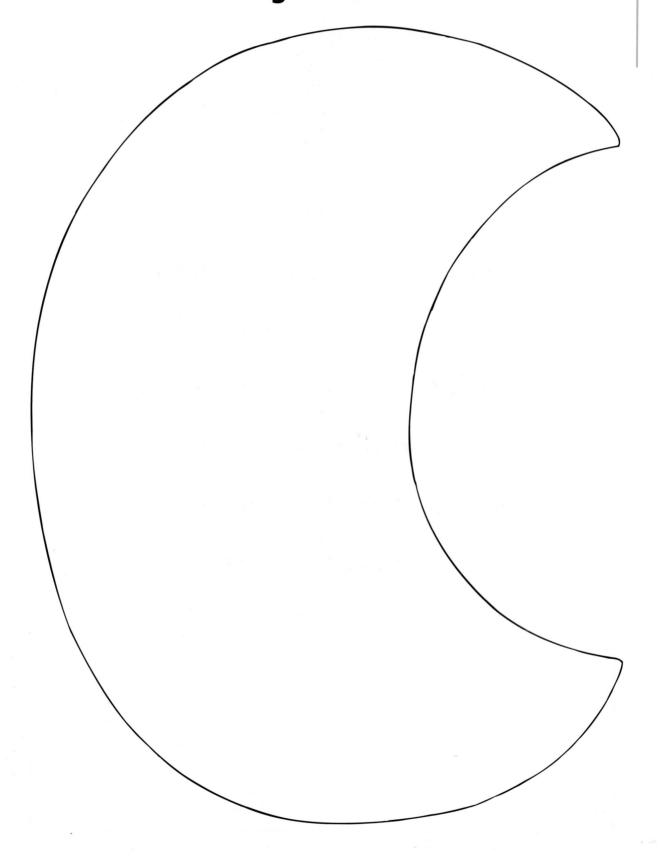